QUALITY
ENGINEERING
STATISTICS

QUALITY ENGINEERING STATISTICS

ROBERT A. DOVICH

ASQ Quality Press
Milwaukee, Wisconsin

Quality Engineering Statistics

Robert A. Dovich

Library of Congress Cataloging-in-Publication Data

Dovich, Robert A.
    Quality engineering statistics / Robert A. Dovich.
      p. cm.
    Includes bibliographical references (p.) and index.
    ISBN 0-87389-141-4:
    1. Quality control — Statistical methods. I. Title.
TS156.D69   1992
658.5'62'015195 — dc20   91-34995
                                                       CIP

109876

ISBN 0-87389-141-4

Acquisitions Editor: Jeanine L. Lau.
Production Editor: Mary Beth Nilles
Marketing Administrator: Susan Westergard
Set in Times by DanTon Typographers. Cover design by Artistic License. Printed and bound by BookCrafters.

For a free copy of the ASQ Quality Press Publications Catalog, including ASQ membership information, call **800-248-1946.**

 Printed on Recycled Paper

Printed in the United States of America

American Society for Quality

Quality Press
611 East Wisconsin Avenue
P.O. Box 3005
Milwaukee, Wisconsin 53201-3005

To Becky, without whose support and assistance, none of this book would have been possible.
She is always first in my book.

CONTENTS

PREFACE

This text provides quality engineers and other professionals with a handy reference to many statistical formulas and techniques. Rather than being theoretical, it assumes that the reader has had exposure to many of these techniques and will use the text as a reference for formulas and fundamental assumptions to perform a particular statistical test.

The bibliography lists several texts that provide the necessary theory and mathematical foundations underlying the statistics covered in this reference. The author recommends that readers understand these principles prior to applying the techniques covered here.

ACKNOWLEDGMENTS

I would like to thank all the people who have assisted me in preparing material for this book. In particular, I want to acknowledge the help of Professors Frank C. Kaminsky and Lawrence M. Seiford of the University of Massachusetts at Amherst for providing the motivation and inspiration for this book.

I am greatly indebted to my wife Becky, who entered all the text into the computer and edited my less-than-eloquent prose. Then, of course, there is Carrie, who always seemed to be there to take the grind out of the process.

POINT ESTIMATES

When performing statistical tests, we usually work with data that are samples drawn from a population or universe. We use the sample data to make estimates about the universe of interest. The first estimate obtained is usually a point estimate.

As we will see in the section on confidence intervals, these point estimates are subject to sampling error and should be interpreted with caution, especially for small sample sizes. The accuracy of the point estimate becomes higher as the sample size gets larger.

There are several point estimates commonly made by quality engineers. Some of these include estimates of central tendency, such as the mean (average), median, and mode. Estimates of dispersion include the variance, standard deviation, and others.

1.1 ESTIMATES OF CENTRAL TENDENCY AND AVERAGE VALUES

Average — The most common measure of central tendency is the average or sample mean. The true (unknown) population mean is denoted by the letter μ, and is estimated by $\overline{X}$. To estimate the parameter μ using $\overline{X}$, we use the following formula:

$$\overline{X} = \frac{\Sigma x_i}{n} \tag{1-1}$$

Using the data shown in table 1.1, estimate the population mean μ by finding $\overline{X}$.

1.45	1.81	1.62	2.27	1.42
2.26	3.52	1.72	1.61	2.43
2.19	0.70	2.03	2.19	2.58
2.51	3.68	3.42	2.28	1.74
1.42	1.33	4.10	1.32	2.25

Table 1.1

$$\Sigma x_i = 53.85$$
$$n = 25$$

$$\overline{X} = \frac{53.85}{25} = 2.154 \text{ or } 2.15$$

Median — Another estimate of central tendency or location is the median. To find the median, we must first place the data in ordered form. Table 1.2 is the ordered form of table 1.1.

0.70	1.45	1.81	2.26	2.58
1.32	1.61	2.03	2.27	3.42
1.33	1.62	2.19	2.28	3.52
1.42	1.72	2.19	2.43	3.68
1.42	1.74	2.25	2.51	4.10

Table 1.2

For odd sample sizes, the median is the (middle) value located at the position of $\frac{n+1}{2}$. For even sample sizes the median will be the halfway point between the two innermost values.

$$\text{Median} = \text{value at } \frac{n+1}{2} \qquad\qquad (1\text{-}2)$$

For the data shown in table 1.2, which has 25 values, n = 25, so the median value is located at the point

$$\frac{25 + 1}{2} = 13$$

The 13th data point has a value of 2.19.

$$\text{Median} = 2.19$$

If the table contained 26 points, the median value location would be calculated as:

$$\frac{26 + 1}{2} = 13.5$$

which would be found as the average of the 13th and 14th points.

Mode — The mode is the most frequently occurring value(s) in a set of data. In our limited data set in table 1.2, the values of 1.42 and 2.19 occur most often (twice each). As a result, our data set has two modes: 1.42 and 2.19.

$$\text{Mode} = \text{most frequently occurring value(s)} \qquad (1\text{-}3)$$

When the population distribution is unimodal and symmetrical, such as in the normal (gaussian) distribution, the values for the mode, median, and mean occur at the same location. When the distribution is skewed, these values diverge, as shown in figure 1.1.

When working with attribute data, measures that are analogous to the average are the proportion or expected numbers of occurrences. For nonconforming product, the fraction nonconforming is estimated by the statistic p, where p is found as:

$$p = \frac{\text{number of nonconforming units}}{\text{number of units tested}} \qquad (1\text{-}4)$$

A more general equation could be written as:

$$p = \frac{\text{number of occurrences}}{\text{total sample size}} \qquad (1\text{-}5)$$

For example, if we test 700 units and find 16 to be nonconforming, the estimate of the population fraction nonconforming would be

$$p = \frac{16}{700} = 0.0228 \text{ or } 0.023$$

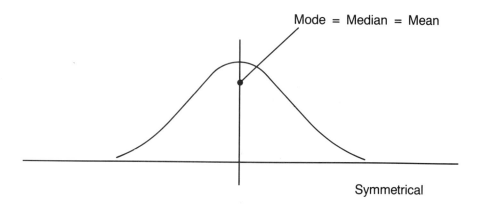

Mode = Median = Mean

Symmetrical

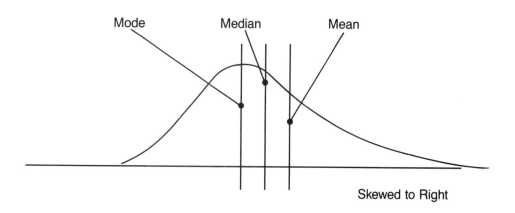

Mode   Median   Mean

Skewed to Right

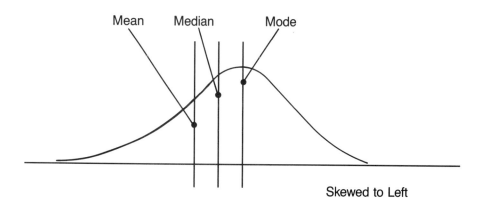

Mean   Median   Mode

Skewed to Left

Figure 1.1

To convert p to a percent value, multiply the result by 100.

$$100 \; (p) = (100)(0.023) = 2.3\%$$

When there are several inspection points per unit, such as in a circuit board, there is a possibility of more than one nonconformance per unit. When the opportunity for occurrence is the same as in identical units, the average number of nonconformances is estimated using the c statistic.

$$c = \frac{\text{number of nonconformances}}{\text{number of items inspected}} \qquad (1\text{-}6)$$

For example, if inspection of 500 circuit boards reveals 1270 nonconformances, the estimate of the number of nonconformances per unit in the population is:

$$c = \frac{1270}{500} = 2.54 \text{ nonconformances per unit}$$

1.2 ESTIMATES OF DISPERSION

This section will focus on the two primary measures of dispersion or variation for individual values. The section on confidence intervals will address measures of variation of averages.

The two principal measures of dispersion are the variance σ^2, which is estimated from sample data by the statistic s^2, and the standard deviation σ, which is estimated by the statistic s. We see that the standard deviation is the square root of the variance.

1.3 VARIANCE AND STANDARD DEVIATION

For variable data, when all values are available, the formula for calculating the population variance is:

$$\sigma^2 = \frac{\Sigma(x_i - \mu)^2}{N} \qquad (1\text{-}7)$$

Where: μ = the population mean

N = the size of the population

The population standard deviation is the square root of the variance.

ESTIMATES FROM SAMPLE DATA

Generally, though, the focus is on using a sample drawn from the population to make inferences about the population. To make an unbiased estimate of the population variance from sample data, the formula is:

$$s^2 = \frac{\Sigma(x_i - \overline{X})^2}{n-1} \tag{1-8}$$

Where: $\overline{X}$ = the mean of the sample drawn

n = the sample size

An algebraically equivalent formula that is easier to calculate is:

$$s^2 = \frac{\Sigma x_i^2 - \frac{(\Sigma x_i)^2}{n}}{n-1} \tag{1-9}$$

To calculate the standard deviation, the square root of the variance is extracted, so we get

$$s = \sqrt{\frac{\Sigma x_i^2 - \frac{(\Sigma x_i)^2}{n}}{n-1}} \tag{1-10}$$

The expected value of s^2, $E(S^2)$ is σ^2, which in effect shows that the sample statistic s^2 is an unbiased estimator of σ^2. For small (fewer than 50) samples, though, the sample standard deviation has an expected value of $C_4\sigma$. Therefore the sample statistic s is not an unbiased estimator of σ.

$$E(s) = C_4\sigma \tag{1-11}$$

To obtain an unbiased estimate of σ from s, we must divide the calculated value of s by C_4. Values of C_4 appear in table F of the Appendix.

Example: Using the data given in table 1.1, calculate the estimate of the population variance and standard deviation from the sample of 25 drawn from the population.

$$\Sigma x_i = 53.85$$

$$\Sigma x_i^2 = 132.15$$

$$(\Sigma x_i)^2 = 2899.82$$

$$n = 25$$

Using formula (1-9), we get:

$$s^2 = \frac{132.15 - \dfrac{2899.82}{25}}{24} = 0.673$$

$$s = \sqrt{0.673} = 0.820$$

For a sample of 25, $C_4 = 0.9896$.

The unbiased estimate of $\sigma = s/C_4$

$$= 0.820/0.9896 = 0.829$$

1.4 MEASURE OF DISPERSION FOR ATTRIBUTE DATA

When working with fraction nonconforming as shown in equation (1-5), the estimate of the variance is a function of the binomial distribution and is given as:

$$s^2 = p(1 - p) \tag{1-12}$$

Using the values following equation (1-5) where $p = 0.023$, we calculate the variance as:

$$s^2 = 0.023(0.977) = 0.0225$$

The standard deviation is the square root of 0.025, or

$$s = \sqrt{0.0225} = 0.15$$

If we are interested in the number of nonconformances per unit or similar count data as in equation (1-6), we may model the variance by the Poisson distribution. When the data can be modelled by the Poisson distribution, the variance is equal to the mean value.

Using the example following equation (1-6), in which the average was 2.54, we find that

$$s^2 = 2.54$$

$$\text{and } s = \sqrt{2.54} = 1.594$$

CONFIDENCE INTERVALS

In section 1.0, we made estimates from a single sample of data drawn from the population. If we were to take another sample from the population, it is likely that the estimates of the mean, variance, and standard deviation would be different, and none would be the exact value of the population parameter.

To compensate for the sampling variation, we use the concept of confidence intervals. These intervals will contain the true but unknown population parameter for the percentage of the time chosen by the engineer. For example, if one were to calculate 95% confidence intervals for the mean, 95% of the intervals calculated from samples drawn from the population would contain the true population mean, while 5% would not.

2.1 CONFIDENCE INTERVAL FOR THE MEAN OF CONTINUOUS DATA

When the sample size is large and the population standard deviation is known or the distribution is normal, we may use the normal distribution to calculate the confidence interval for the mean. The formula is:

$$\overline{X} \pm Z_{\alpha/2} \frac{\sigma}{\sqrt{n}} \tag{2-1}$$

Where: $\overline{X}$ = the point estimate of the average

σ = the population standard deviation

$Z_{\alpha/2}$ = the normal distribution value for a given confidence level (see table A in the Appendix).

Example: Using the data from table 1.1, the estimate of the average is 2.15. If the population standard deviation is known to be 0.8, calculate the 95% confidence interval for the average if the sample size is 25.

From table A, the value for $Z_{\alpha/2}$ is 1.96. The 95% confidence interval is calculated as:

$$2.15 \pm 1.96 \ \frac{0.8}{\sqrt{25}}$$

$$= 2.15 \pm 0.314$$

$$= 1.836 \text{ to } 2.464$$

If the sample standard deviation is estimated from a relatively small (fewer than 50) sample as in the 25 data points in table 1.1, the formula becomes:

$$\overline{X} \pm t_{\alpha/2} \ \frac{s}{\sqrt{n}} \tag{2-2}$$

Where: $t_{\alpha/2}$ = value found in table B in the Appendix for (n-1) degrees of freedom

s = the estimate of the population standard deviation from the sample data

Example: The data in table 1.1 provided an estimate of the mean $(\overline{X})$ of 2.15 and a standard deviation estimate of 0.82. Calculate the 95% confidence interval for the mean. Using formula (2-2) we get:

$$2.15 \pm 2.064 \ \frac{0.82}{\sqrt{25}}$$

$$= 2.15 \pm 0.338$$

$$= 1.812 \text{ to } 2.488$$

2.2 CONFIDENCE INTERVAL FOR THE VARIANCE

Unlike the confidence interval for the mean, the confidence interval for the variance will not be symmetrical about the point estimate, since it is based on the chi-square distribution.

The formula for calculating the confidence interval for the variance, which can then be translated to an interval for the standard deviation by taking the appropriate square roots, is:

$$\frac{(n-1)s^2}{\chi^2_{\alpha/2,\ n-1}} \leq \sigma^2 \leq \frac{(n-1)s^2}{\chi^2_{1-\alpha/2,\ n-1}} \tag{2-3}$$

Where: n = sample size

s^2 = point estimate of variance

$\chi^2_{\alpha/2,\ n-1}$ and $\chi^2_{1-\alpha/2,\ n-1}$ are the table values for (n-1) degrees of freedom

Example: The sample variance (s^2) estimated from the data in table 1.1 is 0.673. Calculate the 90% confidence interval for the population variance.

From table C in the Appendix, the appropriate chi-square value for $\alpha/2 = 0.05$ and 24 degrees of freedom is 36.42, and for $1-\alpha/2$ the value is 13.85. Using formula (2-3) the result is:

$$\frac{(24)(0.673)}{36.42} \le \sigma^2 \le \frac{24(0.673)}{13.85}$$

$$0.443 \le \sigma^2 \le 1.166$$

Based on the single sample of 25, we are 90% confident that the interval from 0.443 to 1.166 contains the true value of the variance.

2.3 CONFIDENCE INTERVAL FOR FRACTION NONCONFORMING — NORMAL DISTRIBUTION

Due to the variability associated with point estimates, any estimates of the fraction nonconforming using the normal distribution are distributed as a second random variable, with the associated confidence interval estimates.

To calculate the fraction nonconforming using the normal distribution, we use equation (2-4):

$$Z = \frac{x - \mu}{\sigma} \tag{2-4}$$

Where: $x =$ any value of interest, such as a specification limit.

Example: The upper specification limit for a process is 90. The process average is 88.5 and the standard deviation is 1.23. Both of these values were estimated from a relatively large sample size ($n = 150$).

Using equation (2-4), calculate:

$$Z = \frac{90 - 88.5}{1.23} = 1.220$$

Using table A, a Z value of 1.220 ($P[Z > 1.220 = 0.111]$) results in a fraction nonconforming of 0.111, or about 11.1%.

In actuality, the estimates of the mean and standard deviation are point estimates. Using these values to estimate fraction nonconforming is intuitively dissatisfying. Instead, the following formulas given by Weingarten can be used to calculate a confidence interval for the fraction nonconforming:

$$Z_{ucl} = Q - Z_{\alpha/2} \sqrt{\frac{1}{n} + \frac{Q^2}{2n}} \qquad (2\text{-}5)$$

$$Z_{lcl} = Q + Z_{\alpha/2} \sqrt{\frac{1}{n} + \frac{Q^2}{2n}} \qquad (2\text{-}6)$$

Where: Z_{ucl} = the Z value for the upper confidence limit

Z_{lcl} = the Z value for the lower confidence limit

Q = the value of Z calculated using the point estimate equation (2-4)

$Z_{\alpha/2}$ = the normal distribution Z value for the approximate confidence level

n = the sample size used in the point estimate

Example: Calculate the 95% confidence interval for the fraction nonconforming using the values from the previous example where the calculated Z value was 1.22.

$Q = Z$ (calculated using equation (2-4)) = 1.22

$Z_{\alpha/2} = 1.96$ for the 95% confidence interval

$n = 150$

$$Z_{ucl} = 1.22 - 1.96 \sqrt{\frac{1}{150} + \frac{(1.22)^2}{300}}$$

$Z_{ucl} = 1.009$

$$Z_{lcl} = 1.22 + 1.96 \sqrt{\frac{1}{150} + \frac{(1.22)^2}{300}}$$

$Z_{lcl} = 1.431$

For $Z_{ucl} = 1.009$, referring to table A, the estimated fraction nonconforming is equal to 0.156 or 15.6%.

For $Z_{lcl} = 1.431$, the estimated fraction nonconforming is equal to 0.0762 or 7.62%.

Therefore the 95% confidence limits on the fraction nonconforming are 0.0762 to 0.156.

2.4 CONFIDENCE INTERVAL FOR PROPORTION

The point estimate for a proportion (or fraction nonconforming) was given in equation (1-4) as

$$p = \frac{\text{number of occurrences}}{\text{total sample size (n)}}$$

When the sample size is large, and n(p) and n(1 - p) are greater than or equal to 5, we can use the normal distribution to calculate the confidence interval for the proportion. The formula for the confidence interval for the proportion is:

$$p \pm Z_{\alpha/2} \sqrt{\frac{p(1-p)}{n}} \qquad (2\text{-}7)$$

Where: p = proportion

n = sample size

$Z_{\alpha/2}$ = normal distribution value for approximate confidence level

Example: Using the values following equation (1-5), calculate the 90% confidence interval for the proportion.

$$p = \frac{16}{700} = 0.023$$

$$n = 700$$

$$Z_{\alpha/2} = 1.645$$

Using equation (2-7), we get

$$0.023 \pm 1.645 \sqrt{\frac{(0.023)\,(0.977)}{700}}$$

$$0.023 \pm 1.645\,(0.0057)$$

$$0.023 \pm 0.00094$$

The 90% confidence interval is the range of 0.014 to 0.032.

2.5 SMALL SAMPLE SIZE CONFIDENCE INTERVALS

When sample size is moderate, the requirements to use equation (2-7) may not be satisfied. In these cases, we may use another set of equations to calculate the confidence interval for the proportion of occurrences in a sample. These equations, adapted from Burr (1974), are suitable with some minor changes made in notations for continuity.

The lower limit Φ_L is calculated:

$$\Phi_L = \frac{2r-1+Z^2_{\alpha/2}-Z_{\alpha/2}\sqrt{[(2r-1)(2n-2r+1)/n]+Z^2_{\alpha/2}}}{2(n+Z^2_{\alpha/2})} \qquad (2\text{-}8)$$

and the upper limit Φ_U is calculated:

$$\Phi_U = \frac{2r+1+Z^2_{\alpha/2}+Z_{\alpha/2} \sqrt{[(2r+1)(2n-2r-1)/n]+Z^2_{\alpha/2}}}{2(n+Z^2_{\alpha/2})} \qquad (2\text{-}9)$$

Where: r = number of occurrences in the sample

n = sample size

$Z_{\alpha/2}$ = two-sided confidence limit value for the normal distribution

Example: In a sample of 50 amplifiers, seven are nonconforming. Calculate the 95% confidence limits for the true fraction nonconforming using these equations. For this example:

$n = 50$, $r = 7$, $Z_{\alpha/2} = 1.96$.

$$\Phi_L = \frac{(2\times7)-1+1.96^2-1.96 \sqrt{[((2)(7)-1)(2)\ (50)\ -((2)\ (7)\ +\ 1)/50]+1.96^2}}{2(50+1.96^2)}$$

$\Phi_L = 0.063$

$$\Phi_U = \frac{(2\times7)+1+1.96^2+1.96 \sqrt{[((2)(7)+1)(2)\ (50)\ -((2)\ (7)\ +\ 1)/50]+1.96^2}}{2(50+1.96^2)}$$

$\Phi_U = 0.274$

The 95% confidence interval for the fraction nonconforming is 0.063 to 0.274. This is compared to the single point estimate of $7/50 = 0.14$.

2.6 CONFIDENCE INTERVAL FOR POISSON DISTRIBUTED DATA

When dealing with the number of occurrences per unit, the point estimate for the average number of occurrences per unit was given in equation (1-6).

To calculate the confidence interval for Poisson distributed data, the relationship given by Nelson between the chi-square distribution and the Poisson distribution allows for simple calculations of Poisson confidence intervals. To calculate the upper confidence limit for number of occurrences, calculate the appropriate degrees of freedom (df) for the chi-square table as $\nu = 2(r + 1)$. To calculate the lower confidence limit for number of occurrences, calculate the df as $2r$.

When calculating 90% two-sided confidence intervals, use the columns labelled 0.05 and 0.95, as well as the appropriate df for upper and lower confidence limits. The value obtained from the chi-square table (table C) is divided by 2 for the required estimate.

Example: An examination of a complex assembly noted 13 nonconformances. Find the 90% confidence interval for the number of nonconformances.

Upper confidence limit df $= 2(13 + 1) = 28$. The chi-square table value for 28 df and $\alpha = 0.05$ is 41.337. The upper confidence limit $= 41.337/2 = 20.67$.

Lower confidence limit df $= 2(13) = 26$. The chi-square table value for 26 df and $1 - \alpha = 0.95$ is 15.379. The lower confidence limit $= 15.379/2 = 7.690$.

Thus, the 90% confidence interval for number of nonconformances is 7.66 to 20.67.

TESTING FOR DIFFERENCES IN MEANS

This section will focus on hypothesis testing for differences in means. In general, sample averages, counts, proportions, etc., will have different values even if they are drawn from a single population. This section will demonstrate methods allowing the user to determine (at the appropriate confidence level) whether the differences noted in the samples are due to sampling variations or to real differences in the population average, count, or proportion.

3.1 TESTING A SAMPLE MEAN VERSUS A HYPOTHESIZED MEAN WHEN σ IS KNOWN

When the standard deviation is known (or can be assumed), the distribution of averages drawn from the population will be distributed normally with a standard deviation of $\sigma/\sqrt{n}$.

Using this information, we can develop hypothesis tests to determine the location (mean) of a population to a hypothesized or historical population mean. The hypotheses that can be tested are:

Two-sided test: $H_0: \mu = \mu_0$
$H_1: \mu \neq \mu_0$

One-sided test: $H_0: \mu = \mu_0$
$H_1: \mu > \mu_0$
or $H_1: \mu < \mu_0$

The reference distribution of the test statistic is the normal distribution, and the formula is:

$$Z = \frac{\overline{X} - \mu_0}{\sigma/\sqrt{n}} \qquad (3\text{-}1)$$

Where: the calculated value of Z is compared to the normal distribution value in table A at the appropriate level of risk (α). (Risk levels are covered in detail in section 5.0.)

Example: To ensure that a new plant has the required capacity to meet demand, it is necessary to maintain the holding time in the bulk tanks to an average of 180 minutes. A similar process is being used at another facility. Using that process as the reference, test whether the holding process averages 180 minutes at the 5% level of risk. The sample size will be 10. Assume the current process has a standard deviation of 3.

$$H_0: \mu = 180 \qquad \alpha = 0.05$$
$$H_1: \mu \neq 180 \qquad n = 10$$
$$Z_{\alpha/2} = \pm 1.96 \qquad \sigma = 3$$

The 10 holding times in the sample are:

$$185, \ 187, \ 187, \ 185, \ 184, \ 185, \ 184, \ 181, \ 180, \ 188$$

$$\Sigma x_i = 1846$$
$$\overline{X} = 1846/10 = 184.6$$
$$Z = \frac{184.6 - 180}{3/\sqrt{10}} = \frac{4.6}{0.95} = 4.84$$

At the 5% level of risk, $Z_{\alpha/2} = \pm 1.96$. Since 4.84 exceeds the value of 1.96, we reject the null hypothesis that the mean is equal to 180 in favor of the alternative hypothesis that the mean is not equal to 180.

3.2 ONE-SIDED TEST — σ KNOWN

In the previous example, it was important to maintain the holding time to an average of 180 minutes to keep the material from premature curing prior to further use.

If the requirement were an average of 180 minutes or less, we would state the null and alternative hypotheses in a different manner, and the result would be a one-sided test with all the risk in one tail of the distribution. We would compare the test statistic to the value of Z_α rather than $Z_{\alpha/2}$.

We would state the hypotheses as:

$$H_0: \mu \leq 180$$
$$H_1: \mu > 180$$
$$\alpha = 0.05$$
$$Z_\alpha = 1.645$$

Again we would use equation (3-1) and compare the calculated value of Z to the value for Z_α of 1.645. As the calculated value of 4.84 exceeds the value of 1.645, we reject the null hypothesis in favor of the alternative hypothesis.

3.3 TESTING A SAMPLE MEAN VERSUS A HYPOTHESIZED MEAN WHEN σ IS ESTIMATED FROM THE SAMPLE DATA

When the standard deviation is unknown and must be estimated from the sample drawn from the population, we use the t distribution to test the observed mean against a hypothesized mean. One of the assumptions of this test is that the sample is drawn from a population that is normally distributed. The formula is:

$$t = \frac{\overline{X} - \mu}{s/\sqrt{n}} \tag{3-2}$$

Example: Use the data from section 3.1 to test the hypothesis that the mean of the population is 183 minutes versus the alternative hypothesis that the mean is not equal to 183 minutes at the 5% level of significance.

H_0: μ = 183 minutes

H_1: μ ≠ 183 minutes

α = 0.05

$\alpha/2$ = 0.025

degrees of freedom (df) = n-1 = 9

$t_{0.025,9}$ = ± 2.262

From the 10-piece sample we find:

$\overline{X}$ = 184.6

s = 2.547

Placing these results into equation (3-2), we get

$$t = \frac{184.6 - 183}{2.547/\sqrt{10}} = 1.987$$

The calculated value of t is 1.987, and the acceptance region for the null hypothesis is the region from −2.262 to +2.262. As a result, there is not enough evidence to reject the hypothesis that H_0 = 183 minutes.

3.4 TESTING FOR A DIFFERENCE IN TWO POPULATION MEANS — STANDARD DEVIATIONS KNOWN

When using samples drawn from two populations to test for differences in their mean values when the standard deviation is known, the reference distribution is the normal distribution, and we use this formula:

$$Z = \frac{\overline{X}_1 - \overline{X}_2}{\sqrt{\sigma_1^2/n_1 + \sigma_2^2/n_2}} \qquad (3\text{-}3)$$

Where: $\overline{X}_1$ = average of the sample drawn from population 1

$\overline{X}_2$ = average of the sample drawn from population 2

σ_1^2 = variance of population 1

σ_2^2 = variance of population 2

n_1 = sample size drawn from population 1

n_2 = sample size drawn from population 2

Example: Using the data given below, test the null hypothesis that the mean of process 1 equals the mean of process 2 versus the alternative hypothesis that the mean of process 2 is greater than the mean of process 1 at the 99% confidence level ($\alpha = 0.01$). Note that this is a one-tail test. Assume the variance of process 1 is known to be 4.3 and the variance of process 2 is known to be 2.5.

Process 1	Process 2
85.2	89.0
87.3	89.4
92.5	90.8
80.8	84.3
84.8	88.2
	88.1

$$H_0: \mu_1 = \mu_2$$

$$H_1: \mu_1 < \mu_2$$

$$\alpha = 0.01$$

$\overline{X}_1 = 86.12 \qquad \overline{X}_2 = 88.3$

$n_1 = 5 \qquad n_2 = 6$

$\sigma_1^2 = 4.3 \qquad \sigma_2^2 = 2.5$

The Z value for the 99% confidence level single-tail test equals 2.326.

Using equation (3-3), we get:

$$Z = \frac{88.3 - 86.12}{\sqrt{(2.5)/6 + (4.3)/5}} = 1.93$$

The Z value calculation of 1.93 is less than the critical value of 2.326, and consequently we do not reject the null hypothesis that the mean of process 1 equals the mean of process 2.

TWO-TAIL TEST

If the alternative hypothesis was $H_1 : \mu_1 \neq \mu_2$, the 1% α risk would be split between both tails of the distribution; the acceptance region would be from -2.576 to $+2.576$; and the test would consist of determining if the calculated Z value is within the range of the critical values (accept H_0) or beyond them (reject H_0).

3.5 TESTING FOR A DIFFERENCE IN TWO POPULATION MEANS — STANDARD DEVIATIONS NOT KNOWN BUT ASSUMED EQUAL

When the population standard deviation must be estimated from samples drawn from two normally distributed populations to test for differences in their mean values, the appropriate reference distribution is the t distribution, and we use this equation:

$$t = \frac{\overline{X}_1 - \overline{X}_2}{s_p \sqrt{1/n_1 + 1/n_2}} \tag{3-4}$$

Where:
$$s_p^2 = \frac{(n_1 - 1)(s_1^2) + (n_2 - 1)(s_2^2)}{n_1 + n_2 - 2} \tag{3-5}$$

The appropriate degrees of freedom for this test is the value in the denominator, $n_1 + n_2 - 2$.

Example: Using the data given in section 3.4, test the null hypothesis that the mean of process 1 equals the mean of process 2, versus the alternative hypothesis that the mean of process 1 is not equal to the mean of process 2 at the 90% confidence level ($\alpha = 0.10$).

$H_0 : \mu_1 = \mu_2$

$H_1 : \mu_1 \neq \mu_2$

$\alpha = 0.10$

$n_1 = 5$

$n_2 = 6$

$t_{\alpha/2, 9} = t_{0.05, 9} = \pm 1.833$

$\overline{X}_1 = 86.12, \ s_1 = 4.272, \ s_1^2 = 18.247$

$\overline{X}_2 = 88.30, \ s_2 = 2.191, \ s_2^2 = 4.8$

Calculating the pooled variance using equation (3-5), the result is:

$$Sp^2 = \frac{(4)\ (18.247)\ +\ (5)\ (4.8)}{5\ +\ 6\ -\ 2} = 10.77$$

Next, calculate the value of t from equation (3-4).

$$t = \frac{86.12\ -\ 88.30}{3.283\ \sqrt{1/5\ +\ 1/6}} = -1.097$$

As this is a two-sided test, we compare the calculated value of t to the critical region of ± 1.833. As -1.097 is within this region, we do not reject the null hypothesis H_0 that $\mu_1 = \mu_2$.

3.6 TESTING FOR A DIFFERENCE IN TWO POPULATION MEANS — STANDARD DEVIATIONS NOT KNOWN AND NOT ASSUMED EQUAL

As mentioned in section 3.5, one assumption of the two sample t test is that of equal standard deviations (variances). When this assumption is not valid, we may use an alternative test outlined by Natrella, the Aspin-Welch test. While it is similar to the two sample t test, there are some distinct differences, the first being the calculation of the degrees of freedom (df).

$$df = \frac{1}{\dfrac{c^2}{n_1-1} + \dfrac{(1-c)^2}{n_2-1}} \tag{3-6}$$

Where:

$$c = \frac{\dfrac{s_1^2}{n_1}}{\dfrac{s_1^2}{n_1} + \dfrac{s_2^2}{n_2}} \tag{3-7}$$

We calculate the t value as follows:

$$t = \frac{\overline{X}_1 - \overline{X}_2}{\sqrt{\dfrac{s_1^2}{n_1} + \dfrac{s_2^2}{n_2}}} \tag{3-8}$$

Example: Two machine tools are set up with similar fixturing and process parameters to determine if the averages of parts machined on the two machines are equivalent. Test to determine if the averages are equal at the 5% level of risk.

$H_0: \mu_1 = \mu_2$

$H_1: \mu_1 \neq \mu_2$

$\alpha = 0.05$

$\alpha/2 = 0.025$

Machine 1	Machine 2
$\overline{X} = 201.8$ mm	$\overline{X} = 203.5$ mm
$s_1 = 4.4$	$s_2 = 2.3$
$n_1 = 12$	$n_2 = 11$

using equation (3-7):

$$c = \frac{\dfrac{19.36}{12}}{\dfrac{19.36}{12} + \dfrac{5.29}{11}} = 0.77$$

and from equation (3-8):

$$df = \frac{1}{\dfrac{(0.77)^2}{11} + \dfrac{(0.23)^2}{10}} = 16.89$$

which will be rounded up to 17.

We find the calculated value for t from equation (3-8);

$$t = \frac{201.8 - 203.5}{\sqrt{\dfrac{19.36}{12} + \dfrac{5.29}{11}}} = -1.175$$

The t value for 17 degrees of freedom and $\alpha/2$ (0.05/2) of 0.025 equals ± 2.110. The critical region for testing the validity of the null hypothesis (H_0) is the region from -2.110 to $+2.110$. Since the calculated value falls within this region, we do not reject the null hypothesis.

3.7 TESTING FOR DIFFERENCES IN MEANS OF PAIRED SAMPLES

When testing for the difference of two means before and after a treatment, we can utilize the paired sample t test. This test could determine if there is a difference in tensile strength before and after a chemical or heat treatment.

The formula for calculating the t value for paired samples is:

$$t = \frac{\bar{d}}{s/\sqrt{n}}$$

(3-9)

Where: $\bar{d}$ = average difference of the paired samples

s = standard deviation of the differences

n = number of pairs

df = number of pairs minus 1

Example: We test 10 employees to determine the time (in minutes) to complete a given task using written instructions. We then give these same employees a video-based training program to determine if such training enables them to perform the task in less time. At the 95% confidence level, test the hypothesis that there is no difference between the time required to complete the task prior to (μ_1) the video training and after (μ_2) the video training.

H_0: $\mu_1 = \mu_2$

H_1: $\mu_1 \neq \mu_2$

$\alpha = 0.05$

$t_{(0.05/2,9)} = \pm 2.262$

Sample No.	Before Video	After Video	Difference
1	27	18	−9
2	17	23	+6
3	22	20	−2
4	26	23	−3
5	26	28	+2
6	30	31	+1
7	20	20	0
8	20	17	−3
9	21	19	−2
10	27	24	−3

$$\bar{d} = \frac{\Sigma d_i}{n} = \frac{-13}{10} = -1.3$$

$$s_d = 3.945$$

$$n = 10$$

Putting these values into equation (3-9), the calculated t value is:

$$t = \frac{-1.3}{3.945/\sqrt{10}} = -1.042$$

The critical region is the area from -2.262 to $+2.262$. The calculated value of -1.042 is within this critical range, so the null hypothesis (H_0) is not rejected at the 95% confidence level, and we conclude that the video-based training did not significantly reduce the time to perform the given task.

3.8 TESTING FOR A DIFFERENCE IN TWO PROPORTIONS

When testing for differences in proportions using large sample sizes, and np and n(1-p) are both greater than or equal to 5, we use the following equations:

$$Z = \frac{p_1 - p_2}{s_{p_1-p_2}} \tag{3-10}$$

The calculation for $s_{p_1-p_2}$ is

$$s_{p_1-p_2} = \sqrt{\hat{p}(1-\hat{p})\,(1/n_1 + 1/n_2)} \tag{3-11}$$

and the value for $\hat{p}$ is

$$\hat{p} = \frac{(n_1)\,(p_1) + (n_2)\,(p_2)}{n_1 + n_2} \tag{3-12}$$

Example: We test two competing emerging technology processes to determine if the fraction of nonconforming product manufactured by each process is equivalent. We draw a large sample from each process. Determine if the fraction nonconforming for each process is the same at the 95% confidence level.

$H_0: p_1 = p_2$
$H_1: p \neq p_2$
$\alpha = 0.05$
$\alpha/2 = 0.025$
$Z_{\alpha/2} = \pm 1.96$

Process 1	Process 2
$n_1 = 300$	$n_2 = 350$
$d_1 = 12$	$d_2 = 21$
$p = d_1/n_1$	$p = d_2/n_2$
$p = 12/300 = 0.04$	$p = 21/350 = 0.06$

Using equation (3-12), calculate $\hat{p}$.

$$\hat{p} = \frac{(300)\,(.04) + (350)\,(.06)}{300 + 350} = 0.051$$

and from equation (3-11), we get:

$$s_{p_1 - p_2} = \sqrt{(0.051)\ (0.949)\ (1/300 + 1/350)} = 0.017$$

We obtain the value of Z from equation (3-10):

$$Z = \frac{.04 - .06}{.017} = -1.176$$

The calculated value of Z falls within the critical value of $\pm\ Z_{\alpha/2}$, which is $\pm$ 1.96. Therefore we do not reject the null hypothesis (H_0) that both of the processes produce at the same level of fraction nonconforming.

3.9 TESTING FOR DIFFERENCES IN COUNT DATA

Equal Sample Sizes — When testing for differences in count data such as nonconformances per unit when the sample size is relatively large, we can perform a test of hypothesis using the normal distribution approximation. The formula is:

$$Z = \frac{|Y_1 - Y_2| - 0.5}{\sqrt{Y_1 + Y_2}} \tag{3-13}$$

Where: Y_1 = number of occurrences in sample 1

Y_2 = number of occurrences in sample 2

0.5 = continuity correction factor

H_0: $\mu_1 = \mu_2$

H_1: $\mu_1 \neq \mu_2$

Example: A check of 10 assemblies noted 260 nonconformances. After investigation and corrective action, a check of 10 assemblies noted 215 nonconformances. At the 95 % confidence limit (α = 0.05), test the hypothesis that the average number of nonconformances per unit is the same before and after corrective action.

H_0: $\mu_1 = \mu_2$ $\alpha = 0.05$

H_1: $\mu_1 \neq \mu_2$ $Z_{\alpha/2} = 1.96$

Calculating the test value of Z using equation (3-13):

$$Z = \frac{|260 - 215| - 0.5}{\sqrt{260 + 215}} = 2.042$$

The calculated value of Z = 2.042 is greater than the value of 1.96. As a result, we reject the null hypothesis in favor of the alternative hypothesis that the average numbers of nonconformances are not equal prior to and after the corrective action.

Unequal Sample Sizes — When the sample sizes are not equal, the equation becomes:

$$Z = \frac{n_2 Y_1 - n_1 Y_2}{\sqrt{n_1 n_2} \sqrt{Y_1 + Y_2}} \tag{3-14}$$

Note the transposition of the sample sizes in the numerator of this equation.

Example: A sample of 40 units noted a total of 67 occurrences of a particular nonconformance. After a design change to aid assembly, a sample of 32 units noted 31 occurrences of this nonconformance. Test to determine if the engineering change resulted in a decrease (one-sided test) at the 90% confidence level.

$$H_0: \mu_1 = \mu_2 \qquad\qquad Z_\alpha = 1.282 \qquad\qquad Y_1 = 67$$
$$H_1: \mu_1 > \mu_2 \qquad\qquad n_1 = 40 \qquad\qquad\quad Y_2 = 31$$
$$\alpha = 0.10 \qquad\qquad\quad n_2 = 32$$

Using equation (3-14), calculate Z as:

$$Z = \frac{(32)\,(67) - (40)\,(31)}{\sqrt{(40)\,(32)}\,\sqrt{67 + 31}}$$

$$Z = \frac{2144 - 1240}{(35.778)\,(9.8995)} = 2.552$$

Since the calculated value of $2.552 > 1.282$, we reject the hypothesis of $\mu_1 = \mu_2$ in favor of $\mu_1 > \mu_2$, and conclude that the design change reduced nonconformances.

3.10 HYPOTHESIS TESTING FOR DIFFERENCES IN MEANS — CONFIDENCE INTERVAL APPROACH

Another approach to testing for differences in two means is the confidence interval approach. If the confidence interval calculated contains the value of zero, the hypothesis that the two means are equal is not rejected. If the confidence interval does not contain zero, the null hypothesis is rejected in favor of the alternative hypothesis.

In section 3.4, we used equation (3-3) to test the hypothesis that two means were equal when the variances were known. We calculated the value of Z and compared it to the Z value for 99% confidence, which is 2.326. As this was a one-sided test, all the risk was put in one tail. This will be equated to a two-sided, 98% (1% in each tail) confidence interval in the following example.

Example: Using the example from section 3.4, calculate the 98% confidence interval for the differences in the two means.

A little algebraic manipulation of equation (3-3) gives this equation for the confidence intervals:

$$\overline{X}_1 - \overline{X}_2 \pm Z_{\alpha/2} \sqrt{\frac{\sigma_1^2}{n_1} + \frac{\sigma_2^2}{n_2}} \qquad (3\text{-}15)$$

From section 3.4, we have:

$$\overline{X}_1 = 86.12, \qquad n_1 = 5, \qquad \sigma_1^2 = 4.13$$

$$\overline{X}_2 = 88.3, \qquad n_2 = 6, \qquad \sigma_2^2 = 2.5$$

The 98% two-sided confidence interval value of $Z_{\alpha/2} = 2.326$.

Using equation (3-15) to calculate the interval gives this result:

$$\text{Interval} = 86.12 - 88.3 \pm 2.326 \sqrt{\frac{4.13}{5} + \frac{2.5}{6}}$$

$$= -2.18 \pm 2.326\,(1.115)$$

$$= -2.18 \pm 2.593$$

$$= -4.77 \text{ to } +0.413$$

Since the confidence interval contains the value of zero (no difference), the null hypothesis of no differences in the means is not rejected. This is the same conclusion drawn in section 3.4.

STANDARD DEVIATIONS UNKNOWN BUT ASSUMED EQUAL

When the standard deviations are unknown but assumed equal as in section 3.5, the formula to calculate the confidence interval for the difference in two means becomes:

$$\overline{X}_1 - \overline{X}_2 \pm t_{\alpha/2,\ df}\ S_p \sqrt{1/n_1 + 1/n_2} \qquad (3\text{-}16)$$

All values in this equation have the same meaning as described in section 3.5.

Example: Using the values calculated in section 3.5, calculate the 95% confidence interval for the difference in the means.

$$\overline{X}_1 = 86.12,\ s_1 = 4.272,\ n_1 = 5$$

$$\overline{X}_2 = 88.30,\ s_2 = 2.191,\ n_2 = 6$$

$$s_p = 3.283$$

$$t_{(.05/2,9)} = 2.262$$

Placing these values into equation (3-16), the confidence interval is:

$$86.12 - 88.30 \pm (2.626)(3.283)\sqrt{\frac{1}{5} + \frac{1}{6}}$$

$$= -2.18 \pm 5.22$$

$$= -7.14 \text{ to } +3.04$$

As the confidence interval contains the value of zero (no difference), we do not reject the null hypothesis of no differences in the means. This is the same conclusion we drew in section 3.5.

TESTING FOR DIFFERENCES IN VARIANCES

There are three common tests for variances: (1) testing to determine if a variance of a population as estimated from a sample equals a hypothesized or known variance, (2) testing to determine if two variances estimated from two samples could have come from populations having equal variances, and (3) testing for the equality of several variances as in an Analysis of Variance (ANOVA).

4.1 TESTING A VARIANCE CALCULATED FROM A SAMPLE TO A HYPOTHESIZED VARIANCE

To test if a variance calculated from sample data equals a hypothesized variance, we use the χ^2 test. The formula is:

$$\chi^2 = \frac{(n\text{-}1)\ s^2}{\sigma^2} \tag{4-1}$$

Where: σ^2 = hypothesized variance

s^2 = variance calculated from the sample data

n = sample size

Example: A process variance has a known variance $(\sigma^2) = 0.068$. A new method of production, suggested to reduce processing time, will be considered if it does not increase the variance. The new method resulted in a variance of 0.087. Using the 5% level of risk (α), test the null hypothesis of no difference in variances versus the alternative hypothesis that the new variance (σ_n^2) is greater than the current process variance (σ_c^2) using a sample size of 12.

H_0: $\sigma_n^2 = \sigma_c^2$

H_1: $\sigma_n^2 > \sigma_c^2$ (one-tail test)

$\alpha = 0.05$

$n = 12$

$df = 11$

Using equation (4-1), the calculated value of χ^2 is:

$$\chi^2 = \frac{(11) \ (.087)}{0.068} = 14.074$$

Since this is a one-tail test, we compare the calculated value of χ^2 to the table value at the 0.05 risk level and 11 degrees of freedom. The table value is 19.675 and is the border of the region for acceptance of the null hypothesis (H_0). Because the calculated value is less than the table (critical values), we do not reject the null hypothesis, as there is not sufficient evidence that the variance from the new process exceeds that of the current process.

4.2 TESTING AN OBSERVED VARIANCE TO A HYPOTHESIZED VARIANCE — LARGE SAMPLES

When the sample size is large, say > 100, we may use a large sample approximation to test a sample variance versus a hypothesized variance. This formula is:

$$Z = \frac{s - \sigma}{\sigma/\sqrt{2n}} \tag{4-2}$$

Where: Z = statistic for comparison to Z_α

Z_α = standard normal curve value

s = standard deviation calculated from sample data

σ = hypothesized standard deviation

n = sample size

Example: Using the values from the example in section 4.1, at the 95% confidence level, with a sample size of 100, determine if $\sigma_n^2 > \sigma_c^2$.

H_0: $\sigma_n^2 = \sigma_c^2$

H_1: $\sigma_n^2 > \sigma_c^2$

Using equation (4-2):

$$Z = \frac{0.295 - 0.261}{0.261/\sqrt{200}} = 1.842$$

Note that in this equation we use the standard deviation rather than the variance.

The one-tail test critical Z value for $\alpha = 0.05$ is 1.645. The calculated value is greater than the critical value, the null hypothesis is rejected, and we conclude σ_n^2 does exceed σ_c^2.

4.3 TESTING FOR A DIFFERENCE IN TWO OBSERVED VARIANCES USING SAMPLE DATA

When comparing the variances of two populations using sample data, the F test is appropriate if both populations are normally distributed. While the t test is less sensitive to small departures from normality, these can significantly affect the risks involved with the F test. Another assumption of this test is that the samples are independent.

The formula for the F test is:

$$F = \frac{s_1^2}{s_2^2}, \; s_1^2 > s_2^2 \tag{4-3}$$

$$df_1 = n_1 - 1$$

$$df_2 = n_2 - 1$$

The larger variance is always placed in the numerator. This results in a one-tail test that simplifies both calculation and interpretation.

Example: Two competing machine tool companies present equipment proposals to a customer. After review of the proposals, a test to determine whether the variances of the product produced by the two machines are equivalent. A sample of 25 units from Machine 1 produced a variance of 0.1211, and 30 units from Machine 2 resulted in a variance of 0.0701. At the 95% confidence level, test the hypothesis that the variances are equal.

$H_0: \sigma_1^2 = \sigma_2^2$ $\qquad\qquad$ $df_1 = 25 - 1 = 24$

$H_1: \sigma_1^2 \neq \sigma_2^2$ $\qquad\qquad$ $s_2^2 = 0.0701$

$\alpha = 0.05$ $\qquad\qquad$ $n_2 = 30$

$s_1^2 = 0.1211$ $\qquad\qquad$ $df_2 = 30 - 1 = 29$

$n_1 = 25$

Placing these calculated values into equation (4-3), calculate the value of F as:

$$F = \frac{0.1211}{0.0701} = 1.73$$

The degrees of freedom (df_1) for the numerator variance = 24 and df_2 for the denominator variance = 29. The F value from table D for 24 and 29 degrees of freedom and $\alpha = 0.05$ is 1.90. As the calculated value of F does not exceed the critical value from table D, we do not reject the null hypothesis (H_0). We conclude there is not enough evidence to state that the variances of product produced by the machines are not equivalent.

4.4 TESTING FOR A DIFFERENCE IN TWO OBSERVED VARIANCES USING LARGE SAMPLES

When the sample sizes are large (> 100), we may use a large sample approximation to the F test. The formula for this approximation is:

$$Z = \frac{s_1 - s_2}{\sqrt{\dfrac{s_1^2}{2\,(n_2-1)} + \dfrac{s_2^2}{2\,(n_1-1)}}} \tag{4-4}$$

Where: s_1^2 = variance of sample 1

s_1 = standard deviation of sample 1

n_1 = sample size of sample 1

s_2^2 = variance of sample 2

s_2 = standard deviation of sample 2

n_2 = sample size of sample 2

Note the switching of sample sizes in the denominator.

Example: Compare the following variances for a significant difference at a risk level of 0.05.

$H_0: \sigma_1^2 = \sigma_2^2$

$H_0: \sigma_1^2 \neq \sigma_2^2$

$\alpha = 0.05$

$Z_{\alpha/2} = \pm 1.96$

$$n_1 = 150 \qquad s_1^2 = 0.13 \qquad s_1 = 0.361$$

$$n_2 = 125 \qquad s_2^2 = 0.07 \qquad s_2 = 0.265$$

Using equation (4-4),

$$Z = \frac{0.361 - 0.265}{\sqrt{\dfrac{0.13}{2\,(124)} + \dfrac{0.07}{2\,(149)}}} = 3.484$$

The calculated value of Z falls outside the critical range of ± 1.96. We reject the null hypothesis in favor of the alternative hypothesis and conclude that $\sigma_1^2 \neq \sigma_2^2$.

4.5 TESTING FOR DIFFERENCES IN SEVERAL OBSERVED VARIANCES

One of the requirements when performing statistical analysis using the Analysis of Variance approach is the equality of variances among all treatment levels. Montgomery outlines one method of testing for equality of variances among the population treatments. Bartlett's test uses the χ^2 distribution with (k-1) degrees of freedom to test the null hypothesis that all variances are equal versus the alternative hypothesis that at least one variance is different. This is illustrated as:

$$H_0: \sigma_1^2 = \sigma_2^2 = \sigma_3^2 = , \ldots , \sigma_k^2$$

H_1: equality does not hold for at least one pair of values of σ_i^2

Bartlett's test calculates the value of χ^2 as:

$$\chi^2 = 2.3026 \,\frac{q}{c} \qquad (4\text{-}5)$$

$$df = k - 1$$

where q equals:

$$q = (N\text{-}k)\log_{10} s_p^2 - \sum_{i=1}^{k} (n_i\text{-}1)\log_{10}s_i^2 \qquad (4\text{-}6)$$

and c equals:

$$c = 1 + \frac{1}{3(k-1)} \left[\sum_{i=1}^{k} (n_i\text{-}1)^{-1} - (N\text{-}k)^{-1} \right] \qquad (4\text{-}7)$$

and S_p^2 is an extension of the pooled variance calculated in section 3.5, and is calculated as:

$$s_p^2 = \frac{\sum\limits_{i=1}^{k} (n_i\text{-}1)\, s_i^2}{N - k} \qquad (4\text{-}8)$$

Example: We draw four samples of six parts each (one sample from each treatment) and calculate the variances of each. The values of the four variances are:

$s_1^2 = 10.96$

$s_2^2 = 9.45$

$s_3^2 = 7.11$

$s_4^2 = 8.10$

$n_1 = n_2 = n_3 = n_4 = 6$

Test for equality of variances at $\alpha = 0.05$.

$H_0: \sigma_1^2 = \sigma_2^2 = \sigma_3^2 = \sigma_4^2$

H_1: at least one variance not equal

$df = k - 1 = 3$

$\chi^2_{.05,3} = 7.815$

The first step is to calculate the pooled variance using equation (4-8):

$$s_p^2 = \frac{(5)(10.96) + (5)(9.45) + (5)(7.11) + (5)(8.10)}{24 - 4} = 8.905$$

Then, using equation (4-6), calculate q:

$$q = (24-4) \log_{10} 8.905 - \sum_{i=1}^{4} (n_i-1) \log_{10} s_i^2$$

$$q = (20) \log_{10} 8.905 - 5[\log_{10} 10.96 + \log_{10} 9.45 + \log_{10} 7.11 + \log_{10} 8.10]$$

$$q = 0.115$$

Then calculate the value for c using equation (4-7):

$$c = 1 + \frac{1}{3(4 - 1)} \left[\frac{4}{5} - \frac{1}{20} \right]$$

$$c = 1 + 1/9(3/4) = 1.083$$

Calculate the χ^2 value using equation (4-5):

$$\chi^2 = (2.3026) \frac{0.115}{1.083} = 0.245$$

The critical value for $\chi^2 = 7.815$. As Bartlett's test is a one-tail test, we compare the calculated value of χ^2 to the critical value. If the calculated value is less than the critical value, we do not reject the null hypothesis. In this case the calculated value of 0.245 is less than the critical value of 7.815, so we conclude the variances are homogeneous.

DECISION ERRORS AND RISKS IN HYPOTHESIS TESTING

5.1 TYPE I AND TYPE II ERRORS

When testing hypotheses, we usually work with small samples from large populations. Because of the uncertainties of dealing with sample statistics, decision errors are possible. There are two types: Type I errors and Type II errors.

A Type I error is rejecting the null hypothesis when it is, in fact, true. In most tests of hypotheses, the risk of committing a Type I error (known as the alpha (α) risk) is stated in advance along with the sample size to be used.

A Type II error is accepting the null hypothesis when it is false. If the means of two processes are, in fact, different, and we accept the hypothesis that they are equal, we have committed a Type II error. The risk associated with Type II errors is referred to as beta (β) risk. This risk is different for every alternative hypothesis and is usually unknown except for specific values of the alternative hypothesis.

We cover these risks in more detail in the section on determining appropriate sample sizes.

D E C I S I O N S		True state of affairs	
		H_0 is true	H_1 is true
	Reject H_0	Type I error	correct decision
	Accept H_0	correct decision	Type II error

Figure 5.1

5.2 ALPHA (α) AND BETA (β) RISKS

There is a given risk associated with each of the errors just described.

ALPHA RISK

The risk of rejecting the null hypothesis when it is true is the alpha (α) risk. The experimenter usually determines the risk before running the test. Common levels of α risks are 0.10, 0.05, and 0.01.

An α risk of 0.05 means that in the long run, the null hypothesis will be rejected when it is true (Type I error) five times out of 100; an α risk of 0.01 means this will happen one time out of 100; and so on.

Tests of hypotheses and the apportionment of the risk usually fall into two categories: one-tail tests where all the risk is in a single tail of the distribution, and two-tail tests where the risk is evenly split between the two tails of the distribution.

The hypothesis for a one-tail test might be stated:

$$H_0: \mu_1 = \mu_2$$

$$H_1: \mu_1 > \mu_2$$

The null hypothesis is that $\mu_1 = \mu_2$, while the alternative hypothesis is that μ_1 is greater than μ_2. As a result, the null hypothesis will be rejected when the value of μ_1 is sufficiently greater than μ_2.

If the standard deviation is known, the test statistic will be calculated as a Z value. If the rejection of the null hypothesis only occurs for values of μ_1 sufficiently greater than μ_2, the null hypothesis will only be rejected when the Z value exceeds a critical Z value for the given risk. If we set the α risk at 0.05, the critical Z value is 1.645 (see figure 5.2). If the calculated value of Z exceeds the critical value for Z, we reject the null hypothesis.

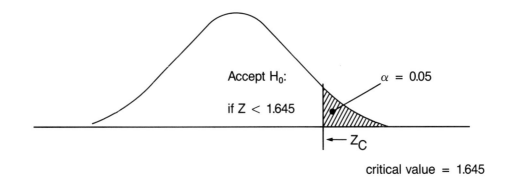

Accept H_0:

if Z < 1.645

$\alpha = 0.05$

Z_C

critical value = 1.645

Figure 5.2

If we stated the alternative hypothesis as H_1: $\mu_1 < \mu_2$, this again would be a one-tail test with all the risk in the lower tail. The critical value for Z with an α risk of 0.05 is -1.645 (see figure 5.3). If the calculated value of Z is less than the critical value, we reject the null hypothesis.

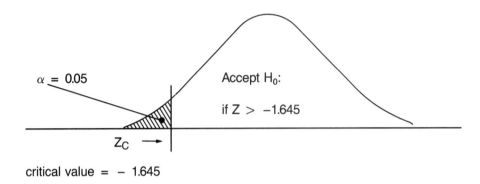

$\alpha = 0.05$

Accept H_0:

if $Z > -1.645$

$Z_C \longrightarrow$

critical value $= -1.645$

Figure 5.3

When we state the hypotheses as follows:

$$H_0: \mu_1 = \mu_2$$

$$H_1: \mu_1 \neq \mu_2$$

the null hypothesis is to be rejected when μ_1 is either significantly larger or significantly smaller than μ_2. In this case, we utilize a two-tail test where the risks are evenly split between the two tails.

If the Z statistic will be used and $\alpha = 0.05$ (as in the one-tail test described previously), there will be 0.025 risk associated with each tail of the distribution. The Z value for 0.025 in the upper tail is $+1.96$. Because the distribution is symmetrical, the Z value for 0.025 in the lower tail is -1.96. Thus there exists a critical range for accepting the null hypothesis at $\alpha = 0.05$. The range is ± 1.96. If the calculated Z value is within ± 1.96, we do not reject the null hypothesis. If the Z value is beyond this range, we reject the null hypothesis in favor of the alternative hypothesis (see figure 5.4).

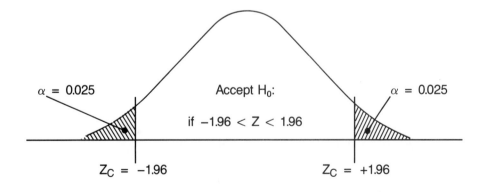

$\alpha = 0.025$

Accept H_0:

if $-1.96 < Z < 1.96$

$\alpha = 0.025$

$Z_C = -1.96$

$Z_C = +1.96$

Figure 5.4

BETA RISK

Beta risk, somewhat more elusive than α risk, is the probability of accepting the null hypothesis when it is false. For example, if the null hypotheses were stated:

$$H_0: \mu = 196$$
$$H_1: \mu \neq 196$$

and the true mean is 197, we should reject the null hypothesis. To calculate the probability of acceptance (risk), we calculate the probability of failing to reject the null hypothesis for a specific alternative hypothesis.

One way to view this risk is to use the confidence interval approach. If the standard deviation is known along with the confidence interval, and the α risk was set at 0.05, the confidence interval for the true mean is:

$$\mu \pm Z_{\alpha/2}\, \sigma/\sqrt{n} \tag{5-1}$$

If $\sigma = 6$, $n = 9$, and $\mu = 196$, we get:

$$196 \pm 1.96\ 6/\sqrt{9}$$

$$= 192.08 \text{ to } 199.2$$

Thus, if the true mean is actually 197, the β risk is the probability that the average of a sample of nine values will fall in the range of 192.08 to 199.2.

If $\mu = 197$, the upper tail probability of rejection is the probability of obtaining a value greater than 199.2. This is calculated as:

$$Z = \frac{199.2 - 197}{6/\sqrt{9}} = 1.10$$

The probability of obtaining a Z value $> 1.10 = 0.136$.

If $\mu = 197$, the lower tail probability of rejection is the probability of obtaining a value less than 192.08. This is calculated as:

$$Z = \frac{192.08 - 197}{6/\sqrt{9}} = -2.46$$

The probability of obtaining a Z value lower than $-2.46 = 0.007$.

The probability of rejection is the sum of the two probabilities just calculated, $0.135 + 0.007 = 0.143$. The probability of acceptance is $1 - 0.143 = 0.857$.

The β risk for $\mu = 197$ equals 0.857. It is possible to calculate a β risk value for each of the infinite number of possible alternative hypotheses. In the section on sample size determination, we will determine the α risk along with a β risk for a specific alternative hypothesis such as $\mu = 197$. From this, we will determine the appropriate sample size for these specific parameters.

CONTINUOUS PROBABILITY DISTRIBUTIONS

6.1 NORMAL DISTRIBUTION

The most commonly known distribution in statistical analysis is the normal distribution. The probability density function (pdf) of the normal distribution is:

$$f(y) = \frac{1}{\sigma\sqrt{2\pi}}\, e^{-(x-\mu)^2/2\sigma^2} \tag{6-1}$$

Some significant properties of the normal distribution include:

1. The curve is symmetrical about the mean value.

2. For a normal distribution, the values for skewness and kurtosis = 0. (Some authors use a kurtosis value of 3 to indicate a normal distribution.)

3. The area from $-\infty$ to $+\infty$ = 1.

4. The mean and standard deviation are independent. This is a necessary and sufficient indicator of a normal distribution.

The mean and standard deviation for the normal distribution using samples drawn from a population are covered in section 1 in equations (1-1) and (1-10).

Some common areas under the normal curve appear in figure 6-1.

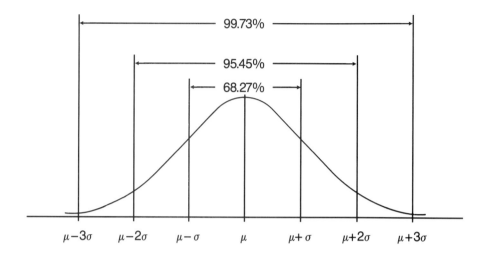

Figure 6-1

68.27% of values will fall within $+/-1\sigma$

95.45% of values will fall within $+/-2\sigma$

99.73% of values will fall within $+/- 3\sigma$

6.2 PREDICTIONS USING THE NORMAL DISTRIBUTION

Predictions using the normal distribution are straightforward and can be made using tables and this formula:

$$Z = \frac{x - \mu}{\sigma} \qquad (6\text{-}2)$$

If the mean value μ is approximated by $\overline{X}$, and σ by s for large samples, we can use this equation:

$$Z = \frac{x - \overline{X}}{s} \qquad (6\text{-}3)$$

Example: The mean of a population is 1.007 with a standard deviation of 0.002. If the upper tolerance limit is 1.010, what will be the fraction nonconforming over high limit? Using equation (6-2), we get:

$$Z = \frac{1.010 - 1.007}{0.002} = 1.5$$

Using table A, the area under the normal curve from $-\infty$ to $Z = 1.5$ is 0.9331. Thus the area beyond $Z = 1.5$ is 0.0668. The fraction nonconforming is 0.0668 or about 6.7%.

Example: If the lower tolerance limit is 1.005, what is the fraction nonconforming below the lower limit? Again using equation (6-2), we get:

$$Z = \frac{1.005 - 1.007}{0.002} = -1$$

The cumulative area under the normal curve from $-\infty$ to -1 is 0.1587. Thus the fraction nonconforming below the lower tolerance limit is 0.1587, or about 15.9%.

6.3 CENTRAL LIMIT THEOREM

The normal curve provides us with significant utility as a result of the central limit theorem. The central limit theorem as given by Duncan states: The form of the distribution of sample means approaches the form of a normal probability distribution as the size of the sample increases.

This theorem is one of the foundations for the use of X-bar charts. Even if the parent population is not normally distributed, the distributions of the averages of subgroups will be reasonably so as the subgroup size increases. This provides us with the symmetrical control limits, as noted by Grant and Leavenworth, and easily calculated probabilities of assignable causes.

6.4 WEIBULL DISTRIBUTION

One of the most versatile distributions for quality and reliability engineering applications is the Weibull distribution. With its changing shapes, the Weibull fits many common distributions. Among these are the Gaussian (normal), exponential, gamma, Rayleigh, and lognormal distributions. The calculations for the scale and shape parameters (to be described later) are somewhat complex, and we will estimate these values using Weibull graph paper.

We will use these parameters with the Weibull distribution:

β = shape parameter; determines distribution shape

η = scale parameter; 63.21% of the values fall below this parameter

Θ = estimated mean; mean time between failures estimate in reliability

$\Gamma(x)$ = gamma function of a variable (x); values of $\Gamma(x)$ appear in table G, along with the equation for calculating the values of $\Gamma(x)$ for large values of x

t = noted time of an individual characteristic

The probability density function for Weibull is:

$$f(t) = \begin{cases} \dfrac{\beta}{\eta} \left(\dfrac{t}{\eta}\right)^{\beta-1} e^{[-(t/\eta)^{\beta}]} & \text{for } t \geq 0 \\[2ex] 0 \text{ for } t < 0 \end{cases} \tag{6-4}$$

and the survival function $P_{(s)}$ is:

$$P_{(s)} = e^{[-(t/\eta)^\beta]} \tag{6-5}$$

Weibull Mean $\mu_w = \eta \Gamma (1 + 1/\beta)$ $\qquad\qquad$ (6-6)

Weibull Standard Deviation:

$$\sigma_w = \eta \sqrt{\Gamma (1 + 2/\beta) - \Gamma^2 (1 + 1/\beta)} \tag{6-7}$$

Example: A unit test reveals that $\eta = 20,000$, $\beta = 2.5$. Calculate the Weibull mean, standard deviation, and $P_{(s)}$ for 10,000 hours.

Using equation (6-6) to estimate the mean:

$$\text{Weibull mean estimate } \hat{\mu}_w = 20,000 \{\Gamma (1 + 1/2.5) \} = 17,746$$

The $\hat{}$ indicates that the value is an estimate of the true population parameter.

Using equation (6-7) to estimate the standard deviation:

Weibull standard deviation estimate $\hat{\sigma}_w$,

$$\hat{\sigma}w = 20,000 \sqrt{\Gamma (1 + 2/2.5) - \Gamma^2 (1 + 1/2.5)} = 7594$$

$$P_{(s)} = e^{-(10,000/20,000)^{2.5}} = 0.838$$

SHAPE PARAMETER — DISCUSSION

The shape parameter (β) is the main influence on distribution shape. When $\Theta = 1$, and the data fits a Weibull distribution with a shape parameter of about 3.6, the distribution has the characteristics of the Gaussian distribution; a shape parameter of 1.0 results in an exponential distribution, while $\beta = 2.0$ is a Rayleigh distribution.

WEIBULL FIT DETERMINATION

Weibull graph paper (see figure 6.2) is a means of graphically displaying life tests and failure times. Weibull graph paper allows us to estimate the shape parameter, scale parameter, and specified percentage of units surviving or failing at a given time.

To plot on Weibull paper, we place the failure times in ascending order and plot them using the rank values from table E for the appropriate sample size.

We draw the best fit line through the data points, then draw a parallel line to the best fit line to determine the shape parameter. The percentage of units expected to survive to a given time reads along the percent axis at the point corresponding with the best fit line. The x axis is the time or cycles to failure.

Example: We test 12 items and record time to failure. The time to failure and median ranks from table E appear in table 6.1. Using Weibull graph paper, determine the scale and shape parameters, as well as the time where 40%, 50%, and 80% of units are expected to fail.

Item No.	Time to Failures (Hrs.) × 100	Median Rank
1	90	5.6
2	116	13.6
3	145	21.7
4	170	29.8
5	185	37.9
6	200	46.0
7	220	54.0
8	265	62.1
9	275	70.2
10	315	78.3
11	335	86.4
12	360	94.4

Table 6.1

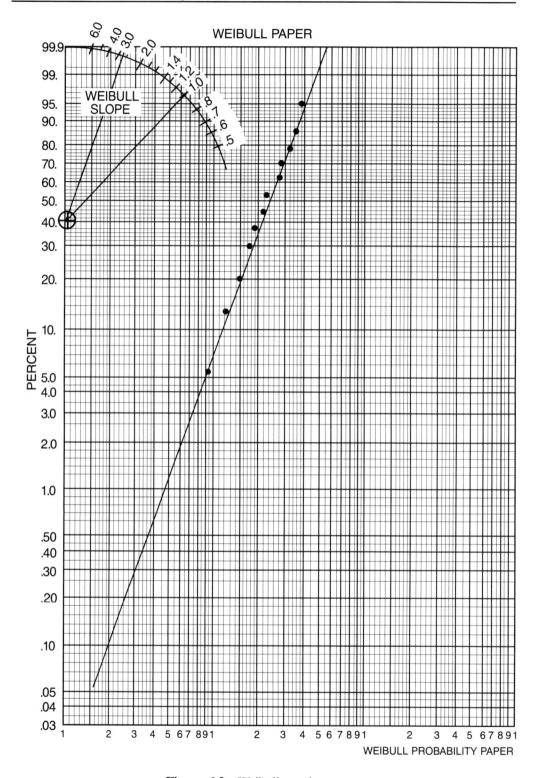

Figure 6.2 Weibull graph paper.

The graph shows that 40% will fail at about 200 hours, 50% at about 222 hours, and 80% at 310 hours. To determine the value for the shape parameter β, draw a straight line from the center point of the circle (next to the 40 on the left side of the graph) that is parallel to the best fit line drawn through the points on the graph. The point of intersection on the Weibull slope semi circle determines the value for the shape parameter. The scale parameter is about 260 hours, and the shape parameter is about 2.70.

The median rank values appear in table E.

To calculate values for median ranks that are not shown in the table, use this formula:

$$MR_{(j)} = \frac{n - j + (0.5)^{1/n} (2j - n - 1)}{n - 1} \qquad (6\text{-}8)$$

Where: n = sample size

j = j_{th} occurrence (failure)

Example: Using the data given above, calculate the value of the median rank for the sixth failure in the sample of 12.

Using equation (6-8):

$$MR_{(6)} = \frac{12 - 6 + (0.5)^{1/12} [2(6) - 12 - 1]}{11} = 0.4596$$

which, when multiplied by 100, equals 45.96%, and has been rounded to 46% in table 6.1.

6.5 LOGNORMAL DISTRIBUTION

When working with continuous distributions that show positive skewness, calculations using the Gaussian (normal) distribution prove inadequate. When this situation occurs, and all values are (or are transformed to be) > 0, taking the natural logs of the values may result in a normal distribution.

For the lognormal distribution:

$$f(x) = \frac{1}{\sigma x \sqrt{2\pi}} \; e^{\,[-1/2 \,(\ln x - \mu/\sigma)^2]} \;, \; x > 0 \qquad (6\text{-}9)$$

The mean and variance of the lognormal are:

$$\text{Mean} = e^{\,[\hat{\mu} + s^2/2]} \qquad (6\text{-}10)$$

$$\text{Variance} = [e^{\,(2\hat{\mu} + s^2)}] \, [e^{s^2} - 1] \qquad (6\text{-}11)$$

Where: $\hat{\mu}$ = mean of the natural logs of individuals

s^2 = variance of natural logs of individuals

Example: We take 25 measurements (in hours) of a component's time to failure. We find the natural logarithms are normally distributed with a mean $\hat{\mu}$ of 3.1 and a variance (s^2) of 1.24 (remember $\hat{\mu}$ and s^2 are for natural log values). Find the untransformed mean and variance in hours.

Using equation (6-10):

$$\text{Mean} = e^{[3.1 + 1.24/2]} = 41.26439$$

Using equation (6-11):

$$\text{Variance} = [e^{2\,(3.1) + 1.24}]\,[e^{1.24} - 1] =$$

$$[1702.750221]\,[2.4556] = 4181.2964$$

To calculate tail area probabilities, we use transformed lognormal values.

$$Z_{\ln} = \frac{\ln(x) - \hat{\mu}}{s} \tag{6-12}$$

Where: $\hat{\mu}$ and s are lognormal values

Example: In the previous example we found that $\hat{\mu} = 3.1$ and $s = 1.11355$. What percentage will survive 50 hours?

Using equation (6-12):

$$Z = \frac{\ln(50) - 3.1}{1.11355} = \frac{3.91202 - 3.1}{1.11355}$$

$$Z = 0.7292$$

Using table A, we find a value of 0.2329, or about 23.29%, will exceed 50 hours.

DISCRETE PROBABILITY DISTRIBUTIONS

7.1 BINOMIAL DISTRIBUTION

Using the binomial distribution is appropriate when there is a series of n trials, and each trial has only two possible outcomes: the occurrence of an event (x) or the nonoccurrence of the event. An example of an occurrence might be a nonconforming item.

Some assumptions when using the binomial distribution are:

1. The probability of an occurrence (x) and a nonoccurrence remain constant from trial to trial.

2. The trials are independent.

The first condition is met when the lot size is infinite or sampling is with replacement. Juran finds this can be approximated in finite populations when the population size is at least 10 times the sample size.

The second condition states that the drawing of a sample and its outcome have no effect on the outcome of any other sample, nor is the sample affected by any previous sample.

When working with the binomial distribution, the probability of an occurrence is designated as p. The probability of a nonoccurrence is (1-p).

$$p = \text{probability of occurrence}$$
$$1\text{-}p = \text{probability of a nonoccurrence}$$

We can generalize the binomial expansion into a general expression that allows the calculation of exactly x occurrences in a series of n trials:

$$P(x \text{ occurrences in } n \text{ trials}) = C_x^n \, p^x(1-p)^{n-x} \qquad (7\text{-}1)$$

Where: $C_x^n = \dfrac{n!}{x! \, (n-x)!}$

p = probability of occurrence

$1\text{-}p$ = probability of a nonoccurrence

n = sample size

x = number of occurrences in n trials

The expected value for the number of occurrences is:

$$E(X) = np \qquad (7\text{-}2)$$

The variance is:

$$Var(X) = np(1-p) \qquad (7\text{-}3)$$

Example: A process has produced nonconformances at a rate of 3% ($p = 0.03$). If a random sample of 25 items is drawn from the process, what is the probability of obtaining exactly 3 nonconforming items?

$p = 0.03$

$1\text{-}p = 0.97$

$n = 25$

$x = 3$

Using equation (7-1), the probability of obtaining exactly 3 nonconforming items is:

$$C_3^{25} \, (0.03)^3 \, (0.97)^{22}$$

$$= \frac{25!}{3!22!} \, (0.03)^3(0.97)^{22}$$

$$= 2300 \, (0.000027)(0.51166) = 0.032$$

The probability of obtaining exactly 3 occurrences in a sample of 25 equals 0.032 or 3.2%.

At times it is necessary to calculate the probability of x or fewer occurrences in a series of n trials. In this case the probability of x or less is the probability of 0 occurrences in n trials plus the probability of 1 occurrence in n trials plus the probability of 2 occurrences in n trials, all the way to x occurrences in n trials. This is shown as equation (7-4).

The probability of x or fewer occurrences in n trials is:

$$P(\text{number of occurrences} \leq x) = \sum_{i=0}^{X} p^x(1-p)^{n-x}, \text{ for } x=0, 1, \ldots, r \quad (7\text{-}4)$$

Example: Using the parameters given in the previous example, calculate the probability of 2 or fewer occurrences in a sample of 25 items.

$$p(0) = 0.467$$

$$p(1) = 0.361$$

$$\underline{p(2) = 0.134}$$
$$\Sigma = 0.962$$

The probability of 2 or fewer occurrences in a sample of 25 = 0.962.

When performing calculations using the binomial distribution, the sum of all possible probabilities of occurrences sums to 1.

As a result, if the previous example asked for the probability of 3 or more occurrences in the sample of 25, we would find that the probability of 2 or less added to the probability of 3 or more sums to 1.

The probability of 3 or more, then, is:

$$1 - P\{2 \text{ or less}\}$$

$$= 1 - 0.962$$

$$= 0.038$$

You can see that this method requires less calculation than if we calculated all probabilities of 3 through 25 and then summed to obtain the result of 0.038.

7.2 POISSON DISTRIBUTION

The Poisson distribution determines the probability of x occurrences over a given area of opportunity. This could be the number of occurrences over a specified time interval, number of nonconformances per assembly, number of customers per day, and so on.

Assumptions that must be met when using the Poisson probability distribution are:

1. The potential number of occurrences must be very large compared to the expected number of occurrences.

2. The occurrences are independent.

Condition 1 is commonly met in practice with nonconformances per assembly, such as the nonconformances per 100 vehicles manufactured. Condition 2 is the same as discussed in the section on the binomial distribution where the occurrence of an event does not affect the probability of occurrence of another event.

The expected number of occurrences is:

$$E(X) = \mu \qquad (7\text{-}5)$$

and the variance of x is:

$$Var(X) = \mu \qquad (7\text{-}6)$$

The Poisson distribution can be generalized into an expression allowing calculation of exactly x occurrences over a given area of opportunity. This expression is:

$$P\{X\} = \frac{e^{-\mu} \mu^x}{x!} \qquad (7\text{-}7)$$

Where: μ = the expected number of occurrences

$\quad$ x = the number of occurrences during this trial

Example: A coil of wire has an average of 7 nonconformances per 10,000 feet. What is the probability of 9 nonconformances in a randomly selected 10,000-foot coil?

Using equation (7-7), we get:

$$p\{9\} = \frac{e^{-7} 7^9}{9!} = 0.1014$$

The probability of 9 occurrences when the expected value is 7 occurrences is 0.1014 or about 10.1%.

If the probability of x or fewer occurrences is necessary, the calculation is similar to that discussed for the binomial distribution in section 7.1. The formula for calculating the probability of x or fewer occurrences in a trial is:

$$\sum_{i=0}^{x} \frac{e^{-\mu} \mu^x}{x!} \qquad (7\text{-}8)$$

Example: Using the values from the previous example, calculate the probability of 2 or fewer nonconformances in a randomly selected 10,000-foot coil.

$$P\{0\} = 0.0009$$

$$P\{1\} = 0.0064$$

$$\underline{P\{2\} = 0.0022}$$
$$\Sigma = 0.0296$$

The probability of 2 or fewer nonconformances when the expected number of nonconformances equals 7 is 0.0296 or 2.96%.

7.3 HYPERGEOMETRIC DISTRIBUTION

When the population size is finite and we draw a series of samples from the population, the probability of occurrence varies from trial to trial, and using the binomial distribution is no longer appropriate.

We use the hypergeometric distribution when there is a series of n trials from a *finite* population, when each trial has only two possible outcomes and we sample without replacement.

We calculate the probability of x occurrences in a sample size (n) from a finite population size (N) containing M nonconformances as:

$$P\{x\} = \frac{C_{n-x}^{N-M} \, C_{x}^{M}}{C_{n}^{N}} \tag{7-9}$$

The expected value of X is:

$$E(X) = n \frac{M}{N} \tag{7-10}$$

The variance of X is:

$$Var(X) = \left[\frac{N-n}{N-1}\right] n \frac{M}{N} \left[1-\frac{M}{N}\right] \tag{7-11}$$

Example: If a lot size of 25 units contains 2 nonconforming items, what is the probability of finding one nonconformance in a sample of 5 units?

Using equation (7-9):

$$P\{1\} = \frac{C_{5-1}^{25-2} C_1^2}{C_5^{25}}$$

$$= \frac{\dfrac{23!}{4!19!} \dfrac{2!}{1!1!}}{\dfrac{25!}{5!20!}} = 0.3333$$

The probability of finding one nonconformance in a sample of 5 from a lot size of 25 containing two nonconformances is 0.3333 or 33.3%.

If the question asked for the probability of one or fewer nonconformances, it would be necessary to calculate the $P\{1\}$ and $P\{0\}$ and add them.

$$P\{1 \text{ or fewer}\} = P\{0\} + P\{1\}$$

$$= 0.6333 + 0.3333 = 0.9667$$

The probability of one or fewer nonconformance in the sample of $5 = 0.9667$ or 96.67%.

7.4 GEOMETRIC DISTRIBUTION

In many cases, the geometric distribution is similar to the binomial distribution as noted by Burr, in that there are n independent trials having two possible outcomes, and the probability of occurrence for each outcome is constant from trial to trial.

The departure from the binomial is that the probability to the first occurrence is of interest (x is fixed) and the value of n varies.

The probability that the first occurrence occurs on the xth trial is:

$$P\{x;p\} = (1-p)^{x-1}p \qquad (7-12)$$

The expected value of X is:

$$E(X) = \frac{1}{p} \qquad (7-13)$$

The variance of X is:

$$\text{Var}(X) = \frac{1-p}{p^2}$$

Example: If the probability of a nonconforming item is 0.02, what is the expected number of samples required to the first failure? Using equation (7-13):

$$E(X) = \frac{1}{0.02} = 50$$

The expected number of trials (samples) to the first nonconforming item is 50.

Example: If the probability of a nonconforming item is 0.02, what is the probability that the first failure will occur on the 100th trial? Using equation (7-12):

$$P\{100;0.02\} = (1-p)^{99}p$$

$$= (0.98)^{99}(0.02) = 0.003$$

The probability that the first failure occurs on the 100th trial is 0.003.

Example: If the probability of failure is 0.01, and five successful trials are required for mission success, what is the probability of mission success?

The probability of mission success is $\{1 -$ the probability of failure in the first 5 trials$\}$. The probability of failure in five or fewer trials is: $P\{1\} + P\{2\} + P\{3\} + P\{4\} + P\{5\}$.

$$P\{1\} = 0.01$$
$$P\{2\} = (.99)\,(.01) = 0.0099$$
$$P\{3\} = (.99)^2(.01) = 0.0098$$
$$P\{4\} = (.99)^3(.01) = 0.0097$$
$$\underline{P\{5\} = (.99)^4(.01) = 0.0096}$$
$$\Sigma = 0.049$$

The probability of the first occurrence in the first five trials $= 0.049$. Thus, the probability of mission success $= 0.951$.

This probability could have also been calculated as the product of 5 successes with a constant probability of 0.99 as:

$$(0.99)^5 = 0.951$$

7.5 UNIFORM DISTRIBUTION

The uniform distribution is not as widely applicable as some of the previously discussed distributions, but it is appropriate in many steady-state applications, such as inventory control, where every state is equally likely.

The expected value for the uniform distribution is:

$$E(X) = \frac{n + 1}{2} \qquad \text{(7-14)}$$

and the variance is:

$$\frac{n^2 - 1}{12} \qquad \text{(7-15)}$$

Where: n = the number of possible outcomes (states)

Example: In an inventory system it is equally probable that there are 1, 2, 3, 4, 5, 6, 7, 8, or 9 items in stock. What is the expected value and variance for this system?

Using equation (7-14):

$$E(X) = \frac{9 + 1}{2} = \frac{10}{2} = 5$$

Using equation (7-15):

$$Var(X) = \frac{9^2 - 1}{12} = \frac{80}{12} = 6.67$$

7.6 NEGATIVE BINOMIAL DISTRIBUTION

The negative binomial distribution has application in determining the probability that the xth occurrence occurs on the nth trial. The probability of an occurrence as in the binomial is designated as p.

The solution to this is equivalent to calculating the probability of x-1 occurrences in n-1 trials and the xth occurrences at the nth trial.

The expected value of X is:

$$E(X) = \frac{x}{p} \qquad \text{(7-16)}$$

and the variance is:

$$Var(X) = \frac{x(1 - p)}{p^2} \qquad \text{(7-17)}$$

To calculate the probability of the xth occurrence on the nth trial, the formula is:

$$C^{n-1}_{x-1} \, p^x (1-p)^{n-x} \qquad \text{(7-18)}$$

Example: The probability of occurrence on any trial is 0.03. What is the probability that the fourth occurrence occurs on the 26th trial?

Using equation (7-18), we get:

$$C_3^{25} \, (0.03)^4 (0.97)^{22} = 0.00095$$

The probability that the fourth occurrence occurs on the 26th trial is 0.00095.

GOODNESS-OF-FIT TESTS

8.1 CHI-SQUARE GOODNESS-OF-FIT TEST

Many tests of hypotheses have certain distributional assumptions such as normal or exponential. To ensure that these assumptions have been satisfied, it is often helpful to perform a goodness-of-fit test.

As there is always variation in sample results from theoretical expectations, we use the chi-square test to test whether the observed results fit the expectation within reason, or whether they depart from expectation to a point that the hypothesized distribution is rejected at the given significance level.

The chi-square test is a test of hypothesis where the hypothesis (what is the assumed distribution) is developed, the level of significance is determined, the expected frequencies are calculated, and observed frequencies are compared to expected frequencies. When using the chi-square test, the expected number in any single interval should be at least 5.

The formula for calculating the chi-square test statistic for this one-tail test is:

$$\chi^2 = \frac{\Sigma(O_i\text{-}E_i)^2}{E_i} \tag{8-1}$$

Where: O_i = the observed frequency in a given interval

E_i = the expected frequency in a given interval

The degrees of freedom for this test are:

$$df = k - m - 1$$

where k is the number of intervals or cells and m is the number of parameters *estimated* from the sample data. For example, if the test is that the distribution is a normal distribution with a mean (μ) of 10 and a standard deviation (σ) of 1, these are given parameters, and sample estimates are not necessary. As a result, the degrees of freedom value is k - 1.

If we are only testing whether the data fit a normal distribution, we calculate the expected values using estimates for the mean ($\overline{X}$) and standard deviation (s). These estimates reduce the available degrees of freedom by 1 each. The degrees of freedom for this case is k - 2 - 1, or k - 3.

Example: It is believed that the time between machine breakdowns follows the exponential distribution. We track a bank of identical machines for number of hours between breakdowns. Test the hypothesis that the distribution is exponential using the 95% (α = 0.05) level of confidence.

H_0: distribution is exponential

H_1: distribution is not exponential

$\alpha = 0.05$

The data are shown grouped in intervals of 100 hours in table 8.1.

Time Between Breakdowns x 100 (Interval)							
Interval	0-1	>1-2	>2-3	>3-4	>4-5	>5-6	>6
Number of Breakdowns	325	180	63	53	33	18	6

Table 8.1

The average time to breakdown was estimated from the sample of 678 to be 156.6 hours, and $\lambda = \dfrac{1}{156.6} = 0.0064$.

The expected values for each interval appear in table 8.2.

Interval	Probability - pi		Expected Value npi
0 - 100	$e^0-e^{-0.0064(100)}$	= 0.4727	320.5
>100 - 200	$e^{-0.0064(100)}-e^{-0.0064(200)}$	= 0.2493	169.0
>200 - 300	$e^{-0.0064(200)}-e^{-0.0064(300)}$	= 0.1314	89.1
>300 - 400	$e^{-0.0064(300)}-e^{-0.0064(400)}$	= 0.0693	47.0
>400 - 500	$e^{-0.0064(400)}-e^{-0.0064(500)}$	= 0.0365	24.7
>500 - 600	$e^{-0.0064(500)}-e^{-0.0064(600)}$	= 0.0193	13.1
>600	$e^{-0.0064(600)}$	= 0.0215	14.6
		$\Sigma = 1.0000$	678.0

Table 8.2

Using equation (8-1) and the value from tables 8.1 and 8.2, we calculate χ^2 as:

$$\chi^2 = \frac{(325 - 320.5)^2}{320.5} + \frac{(180 - 169)^2}{169} + \frac{(63 - 89.1)^2}{89.1} + \frac{(53 - 47)^2}{47}$$

$$+ \frac{(33 - 24.7)^2}{24.7} + \frac{(18 - 13.1)^2}{13.1} + \frac{(6 - 14.6)^2}{14.6} = 18.878$$

The degrees of freedom is computed as the number of intervals minus the number of parameters estimated (which is 1, as the mean was estimated from the sample), minus 1.

$$df = 7 - 1 - 1 = 5$$

The χ^2 value for $\alpha = 0.05$ and 5 degrees of freedom is 11.07. The calculated value of χ^2 is 18.878, which exceeds the critical value of 11.07 from the table. Therefore we reject the null hypothesis (H_0) that the time to breakdown for this style of equipment is modeled by the exponential distribution.

8.2 TEST OF NORMALITY USING SKEWNESS AND KURTOSIS

Skewness is a measure of symmetry. A skewness value of 0 indicates a symmetrical distribution. A positive value of skewness indicates that the distribution has a longer tail to the right of the mean, while a negative value of skewness indicates a longer tail to the left.

The kurtosis measure compares the grouping of values about the mean to the weight or heaviness of the area in the tail. A large value of kurtosis indicates a high concentration about the mean with relatively thin tails, while a negative value of kurtosis indicates a lower concentration about the mean with relatively heavier tails — that is, the probability falls toward zero more slowly.

While the following values are not necessary and sufficient to determine if a distribution is normal, we know that the normal distribution has values for skewness and kurtosis, as noted in section 6.1 (skewness and kurtosis = 0). Some authors use a kurtosis value of 3 to indicate a normal distribution, rather than 0 as used here.

$$\text{skewness} = \frac{m_3}{m_2^{3/2}} \qquad (8\text{-}2)$$

$$\text{kurtosis} = \frac{m^4}{m_2^{\,2}} - 3 \qquad (8\text{-}3)$$

Where: m_2 = second moment about the mean

m_3 = third moment about the mean

m_4 = fourth moment about the mean

The values of m_2, m_3, and m_4 are estimated by:

$$m_2 = \frac{\Sigma(x_i - \overline{X})^2}{n} \qquad (8\text{-}4)$$

$$m_3 = \frac{\Sigma(x_i - \overline{X})^3}{n} \qquad (8\text{-}5)$$

$$m_4 = \frac{\Sigma(x_i - \overline{X})^4}{n} \qquad (8\text{-}6)$$

When the sample size is very large, we can use the normal distribution to test the hypothesis that the values calculated from a sample came from a normal distribution, as these values are symmetrical about 0.

For large samples, the standard deviation of the estimate for skewness is $\sqrt{6/n}$ and the standard deviation for the estimate of kurtosis is $\sqrt{24/n}$.

To calculate a Z value for skewness, use this formula:

$$Z = \frac{\text{skewness}}{\sqrt{6/n}} \qquad (8\text{-}7)$$

The Z value for kurtosis is:

$$Z = \frac{\text{kurtosis}}{\sqrt{24/n}} \qquad (8\text{-}8)$$

Since these tests of hypothesis are two-sided, the $Z\alpha$ values for 95% confidence are $\pm$ 1.96, and for 90% confidence the values are $\pm$ 1.645.

Example: A sample of 500 units resulted in estimates of 0.29 for skewness and of -0.14 for kurtosis. Test the hypothesis that these values could have resulted from a normal distribution at the 95% level of confidence ($\alpha = 0.05$).

Using equation (8-7) to test the estimate of skewness:

$$Z = \frac{0.29}{\sqrt{6/500}} = 2.647$$

Using equation (8-8) to test the estimate of kurtosis:

$$Z = \frac{-0.14}{\sqrt{24/500}} = -0.639$$

As the calculated Z value for skewness of 2.747 is beyond the critical $Z\alpha$ range of $\pm$ 1.96, we reject the hypothesis that the distribution is symmetrical and conclude that it is skewed to the right.

Since the calculated Z value for kurtosis is within the critical range of $\pm$ 1.96, we do not reject the hypothesis that kurtosis equals zero. Even though the estimate from the sample was not zero, there is not enough evidence to state at the given level of confidence that it is not zero.

For smaller sample sizes, see table A19 in the text by Snedecor and Cochran to test the hypotheses for skewness and kurtosis. When using this table, note that the authors do not subtract the value of 3 from equation (8-3) and that they use a kurtosis value of 3 for a normal distribution.

9.0 SAMPLE SIZE DETERMINATION FOR TESTS OF HYPOTHESES

Sometimes, when testing for a difference in a population mean versus a hypothesized mean, or when testing two population means, controlling only the α risk is not sufficient. For example, if the processing cost on a part is very high and a small but real reduction in processing time can save considerable costs, we want to ensure that our test reveals this reduction.

If the processing time averages 28 hours with a standard deviation of 1½ hours, a 1½-hour reduction in processing time (a difference of 1 standard deviation) with no change in variation would result in a 5.4% savings in time as well as other cost savings. If this is the case, it would be beneficial to set a low risk, called beta (β), of not detecting a change as small as one standard deviation.

In these situations, we must determine in advance the α and β risks and the difference to detect in units of standard deviation. Then, using equations from Natrella, we can determine the sample size required to ensure that these levels of risk are maintained.

Relatively few equations will be expanded or modified to determine the required sample size. The difference in means that are tested in the hypothesis at a given β risk will be in the number of standard deviations. The progression of this section will follow that of section 3.0.

ACKNOWLEDGMENT

While the majority of these equations are in general use and appear in many publications, all of the equations used in this section were drawn or adapted from the text by Mary Gibbons Natrella. The author recommends this text to anyone having more than a passing interest in experimental statistics.

9.1 SAMPLE SIZE REQUIRED TO TEST AN OBSERVED MEAN VERSUS A HYPOTHESIZED MEAN WHEN σ IS KNOWN

We will cover two facets: the first equation will be for two-tail tests where the direction of difference is not important, and the next equation will cover one-tail tests.

TWO-TAIL TEST

When performing a two-tail test, we must determine the difference in standard deviation units (d).

$$d = \left| \frac{\mu_H - \mu_0}{\sigma} \right| \qquad (9\text{-}1)$$

Where: μ_H = the mean value that we want to detect at the given level of risk

μ_0 = the hypothesized mean

σ = standard deviation

The required sample size for the test is:

$$n = \frac{(Z_{1-\alpha/2} + Z_{1-\beta})^2}{d^2} \qquad (9\text{-}2)$$

Where: $Z_{1-\alpha/2}$ = Z value determined by α

$Z_{1-\beta}$ = Z value determined by β

Example: The current process has an average of 1.500 and a standard deviation of 0.06. A new method of processing is proposed, but a change in the process average of 0.024 in either direction would be detrimental, and we would like to detect a shift of this magnitude with 95% confidence. $\beta = 0.05$ and $\alpha = 0.05$.

Using equation (9-1):

$$d = \left| \frac{1.524 - 1.500}{0.06} \right| \text{ or } \left| \frac{1.476 - 1.500}{0.06} \right| = 0.40$$

Using equation (9-2), the sample size n is:

$$n = \frac{(1.96 + 1.645)^2}{(0.40)^2} = 81.23 \text{ or } 82$$

Rounding to the next highest value if the result is not an integer is recommended.

ONE-TAIL TEST

The one-tail test equations are very similar to the two-tail. The major difference is that the value $Z_{1-\alpha/2}$ becomes $Z_{1-\alpha}$. The value of d is calculated as in equation (9-1). The sample size calculation is:

$$n = \frac{(Z_{1-\alpha} + Z_{1-\beta})^2}{d^2} \qquad (9\text{-}3)$$

Example: In the previous problem, consider the alternative hypothesis as: the process will be considered unacceptable if the average value decreases by a value of 0.024. We are not concerned if the process changes to a value greater than 1.500, and we ignore any changes above 1.500. Keeping all other parameters constant, calculate the sample size required to detect this one-directional (single-tail) shift.

From equation (9-1), we get:

$$\left| \frac{1.476 - 1.500}{0.06} \right| = 0.40$$

and from equation (9-3), we get:

$$n = \frac{(1.645 + 1.645)^2}{(.40)^2} = 67.65 \text{ or } 68$$

9.2 SAMPLE SIZE REQUIRED TO TEST AN OBSERVED MEAN VERSUS A HYPOTHESIZED MEAN WHEN σ IS ESTIMATED FROM OBSERVED VALUES

When estimating the standard deviation from the sample data, the t test is the appropriate test of hypothesis. Equations (9-1) through (9-3) are the same except for the addition of a constant for α risks of 0.05 and 0.01. These constants from Natrella appear in table 9.1.

Two-Tail Test	Constant
If $\alpha = 0.01$	Add 4 to calculated sample size
If $\alpha = 0.05$	Add 2 to calculated sample size
If $\alpha \geq 0.10$	None required
One-Tail Test	**Constant**
If $\alpha = 0.01$	Add 3 to calculated sample size
If $\alpha = 0.05$	Add 2 to calculated sample size
If $\alpha \geq 0.10$	None required

Table 9.1

9.3 SAMPLE SIZE REQUIRED TO TEST FOR DIFFERENCES IN σ TWO OBSERVED MEANS WHEN STANDARD DEVIATION FOR EACH POPULATION IS KNOWN

TWO-TAIL TEST

The method of testing is that described in section 3.4. The first step is to calculate the value of d. The formula is:

$$d = \frac{\mu_1 - \mu_2}{\sqrt{\sigma_1^2 + \sigma_2^2}}$$
(9-4)

We then calculate the required sample sizes:

$$n = \frac{(Z_{1-\alpha/2} + Z_{1-\beta})^2 + 2}{d^2}$$
(9-5)

Example: We are using two processes to manufacture a product. As the product streams are mixed at a later point, we determine that a difference in the two averages $|\mu_1 - \mu_2|$ of 0.024 or greater is unacceptable. If the standard deviation (σ_1) of process 1 = 0.0714, and the standard deviation (σ_2) of process 2 = 0.06, determine the required (equal for each process) sample sizes to detect a difference as low as 0.024 with $\alpha = 0.05$ and $\beta = 0.10$.

Using equation (9-4), d is calculated as:

$$d = \frac{0.024}{\sqrt{(0.0714)^2 + (0.06)^2}}$$

and from equation (9-5), $n = n_1 = n_2$:

$$n = \frac{(1.96 + 1.282)^2 + 2}{(0.257)^2} = 161.1 \text{ or } 162$$

Thus the sample size from each process is to be 162:

$$n = n_1 = n_2 = 162.$$

ONE-TAIL TEST

When the direction of difference between the two sample averages is important, we calculate n using equation (9-6) and calculate d using equation (9-4).

$$n = \frac{(Z_{1-\alpha} + Z_{1-\beta})^2}{d^2} + 2$$
(9-6)

Example: If, in the previous example, it was important to test whether the mean of process 1 is greater than the mean of process 2 with all other values equal, we would get:

d = 0.257

Using equation (9-6):

$$n = \frac{(1.645 + 1.282)^2}{(0.257)^2} + 2 = 131.7 \text{ or } 132$$

$$n = n_1 = n_2 = 132$$

9.4 SAMPLE SIZE REQUIRED TO TEST FOR DIFFERENCES IN σ TWO OBSERVED MEANS WHEN ESTIMATED FROM THE OBSERVED DATA

This procedure is the same as that described in section 9.2. Use the values given in that section.

9.5 PAIRED SAMPLE t TEST REQUIREMENTS

The sample sizes calculated in this section are for performing the test described in section 3.10.

TWO-TAIL TEST

When performing the paired sample t test, the estimate of the standard deviation of the difference will result from the paired sample. In many cases a preliminary test will provide an estimate of σ from s, and this will enable us to calculate the required number of pairs for the necessary precision sought in the test.

To determine the value for d, use the following equation:

$$d = \left| \frac{\mu_1 - \mu_2}{s} \right| \tag{9-7}$$

We then calculate the sample size n using equation (9-2), and adjust with the constants from table 9.1.

Example: We believe that the heat treatment of a process will change the size of a part by 0.024 or less. A preliminary sample of part sizes measured before and after heat treatment estimated the standard deviation of the paired differences to be 0.06. How large a sample is required to detect a difference in the averages of the paired values as low as 0.024 with an α level = 0.05 and a β level = 0.05?

Using equation (9-7) for d:

$$d = \frac{0.024}{0.06} = 0.40$$

The sample size equation is:

$$n = \frac{(Z_{1-\alpha/2} + Z_{1-\beta})^2}{d^2} + \text{constant from table 9.1} \qquad (9-8)$$

For this example:

$$n = \frac{(1.96 + 1.645)^2}{(0.40)^2} = 81.23 + \text{constant}$$

$$n = 81.23 \text{ or } 82 + \text{constant}$$

The constant value for a two-tail test and $\alpha = 0.05$ is 2. The resulting number of paired samples is $82 + 2 = 84$.

ONE-TAIL TEST

If the direction of difference is important ($\mu_1 < \mu_2$ or $\mu_1 > \mu_2$), we use a one-tail test. To compute the sample size, use equation (9-7) to calculate the value of d. Then calculate the sample size as follows:

$$n = \frac{(Z_{1-\alpha} + Z_{1-\beta})^2}{d^2} + \text{constant from table 9.1} \qquad (9-9)$$

Example: If, instead of a two-tail test, it is important that part size does not increase by 0.024 with all other parameters being the same, what is the required number of paired samples to detect a one-directional shift of 0.024?

Using equation (9-7) for d, the value is the same: 0.40.

From equation (9-9), the sample size is:

$$n = \frac{(1.645 + 1.645)^2}{(0.40)^2} + \text{constant from table 9.1}$$

$$n = 67.65 \text{ or } 68 + \text{constant}$$

As $\alpha = 0.05$, the constant value is 2, and the required number of sampled pairs is $68 + 2 = 70$.

9.6 SAMPLE SIZE REQUIRED FOR CHI-SQUARE TEST OF OBSERVED VARIANCE TO A HYPOTHESIZED VARIANCE

When performing the chi-square test outlined in section 4.1, there are two conditions of interest for the alternative hypothesis. These alternatives are:

$$1. \ \sigma_n^2 > \sigma_c^2$$

$$2. \ \sigma_n^2 < \sigma_c^2$$

Where: σ_c^2 = current or hypothesized variance

σ_n^2 = new or observed variance from sample data

As with the previous methods in this section, from Natrella we get equations for both cases.

Case 1. When performing a chi-square test in case 1, we must specify the differences in variances we wish to detect at a given risk (β). We will divide this larger standard deviation by the hypothesized standard deviation to determine a ratio (R). Note that we use the standard deviations rather than the variance to calculate the ratio.

$$R = \frac{\sigma_n}{\sigma_c} \tag{9-10}$$

We calculate the sample size for a given value of R, α, and β as

$$n = 1 + \frac{1}{2}\left[\frac{Z_{1-\alpha} + R(Z_{1-\beta})}{R - 1}\right]^2 \tag{9-11}$$

Example: A process is operating with a standard deviation of 0.0012. A new lower cost process is proposed, but it will not be considered acceptable if the variability increases by more than 25%. Using the values of $\alpha = 0.05$ and $\beta = 0.10$ in detecting this increase to a standard deviation of 0.0015, calculate the sample size necessary to perform the chi-square test.

Using equation (9-10):

$$R = \frac{0.0015}{0.0012} = 1.25$$

We calculate the sample size using equation (9-11):

$$n = 1 + \frac{1}{2}\left[\frac{1.645 + 1.25(1.282)}{1.25 - 1}\right]^2 = 85.37 \text{ or } 86$$

The sample size necessary to perform the chi-square test to determine if the new variance is greater than the current variance by a difference of 25% (which is case 1) with the given risks is 86.

Case 2. When testing that the new variance is less than the current variance, the ratio (R) is calculated as in equation (9-10) and will be less than 1. The difference in the methods is that the denominator in equation (9-11) changes from R -1 to 1- R, as shown:

$$n = 1 + \frac{1}{2}\left[\frac{Z_{1-\alpha} + R(Z_{1-\beta})}{1 - R}\right]^2 \tag{9-12}$$

Example: If, in the previous example, the new process were more expensive and would be adopted if the decrease in variability were 25% and all other risks remain the same, we get:

$$R = \frac{0.0009}{0.0012} = 0.75$$

Using equation (9-12), n is calculated:

$$n = 1 + \frac{1}{2}\left[\frac{1.645 + 0.75(1.282)}{0.25}\right]^2 = 55.35 \text{ or } 56$$

The sample size necessary to perform the chi-square test to determine if the new variance is less than the current variance (case 2) by 25% with the given risk is 56.

9.7 SAMPLE SIZE REQUIRED FOR F TEST OF TWO OBSERVED VARIANCES

The F test for testing for the difference in two observed (sample) variances was described in section 4.3. As with the chi-square test, it may be of interest to detect a specific difference between two variances at a given level of risk (β). For this method to be used, the two process sample sizes must be equal.

As in the previous section, we will calculate (R) which again uses the standard deviation in place of the variance:

$$R = \frac{\sigma_1}{\sigma_2}, \text{ where } \sigma_1 > \sigma_2 \tag{9-13}$$

Once we have calculated the ratio and determined the α and β risks, the sample size required to detect the difference noted by the ratio is:

$$n = 2 + \left[\frac{Z_{1-\alpha} + Z_{1-\beta}}{\ln R}\right]^2 \tag{9-14}$$

Example: Two processes are combined into one process stream. If the standard deviation of the processes differ by more than 30% ($\sigma_1 > 1.3\,\sigma_2$), the effects on the downstream variation are detrimental. Determine the sample sizes (which will be the same) to detect a difference of this magnitude with a β risk of 0.10. Set the α risk at 0.05.

The value of R determined in the example description was 1.3.

We calculate the sample sizes $n = n_1 = n_2$ from equation (9-14) as:

$$n = 2 + \left[\frac{1.96 + 1.645}{0.262}\right]^2 = 191.3 \text{ or } 192$$

The sample size from each process is 192.

ANALYSIS OF VARIANCE

In this section, we will focus on the mainstream Analysis of Variance methods of one-way ANOVA, two-way ANOVA, and two-way ANOVA with replications. Factors above the two-way level are simply extensions of the two-level model. All examples will be for fixed rather than random treatment levels, followed by a single random effects/components of variance model.

We use the fixed model to test all levels of interest in the experiment. When the chosen levels of the factor are the only levels under consideration, we use a fixed effects model.

We use the random effects model when choosing a relatively small number of possible levels for the model and wish to determine how much variability is contributed by these factors to the total amount of variability captured. This will become more apparent in forthcoming examples.

10.1 ASSUMPTIONS FOR ANOVA

We must meet several assumptions about the distributions of the factors at different levels to maintain the prescribed α risk:

The main assumptions are:

1. The distributions of outputs for all treatment levels follow the normal distribution.

2. The variances of all treatment levels are equal. We can test this assumption using Bartlett's test (discussed in section 4.5).

3. All samples are random samples from their respective populations and are independent.

10.2 ONE-WAY ANOVA — FIXED EFFECTS MODEL

We use the one-way fixed effects model to determine if the averages among different treatment levels are equal, or if there is reasonable evidence that at least one treatment average is different from the others. In a completely randomized design (the type discussed here), treatments are applied to samples in a random order. The one-way ANOVA table appears as table 10.1

ANOVA Table					
Source	Sum of Squares	Degrees of Freedom	Mean Square	F	Prob. > F
Between Treatments	SST	a - 1	$\dfrac{SST}{a-1}$	$\dfrac{MST}{MSE}$	
Error	SSE	N - a	$\dfrac{SSE}{N-a}$	—	
Total	TSS	N - 1	—	—	

Table 10.1

Where: SST = sum of squares between the treatment levels

SSE = sum of squares due to error

TSS = total sum of squares

N = total number of tests run

a = number of treatments

MST = treatment mean square = SST/a-1

MSE = error mean square = SSE/N-a

The formulas for the sums of squares are:

$$SST = \sum_{j=1}^{a} \frac{y_{.j}^2}{n} - \frac{Y_{..}^2}{N} \qquad (10\text{-}1)$$

$$TSS = \sum_{i=1}^{a} \sum_{j=1}^{n} y_{ij}^2 - \frac{Y_{..}^2}{N} \qquad (10\text{-}2)$$

$$SSE = TSS - SST \qquad (10\text{-}3)$$

Where: $Y_{.j}$ = sum of column J

Y.. = sum of all values for all tests

The next-to-last column in the ANOVA table is labelled F. The Analysis of Variance compares averages by calculating estimates of the variance from two sources: (1) the variance calculated from the differences in averages between treatments, and (2) the pooled variances calculated from variation within treatments.

If the treatment averages are all equal, these two estimates will be very nearly equal, and an average F value of 1 will result if the MST is divided by MSE. If the treatments result in different averages, the value for MST will be larger than MSE, and the F value will increase. If the F value gets large enough, the null hypothesis (stated below) will be rejected in favor of the alternative hypothesis. The degrees of freedom for the F test are a-1, N-a.

The hypotheses for this test are:

$$H_0: \mu_1 = \mu_2 = \ldots = \mu_a$$

$$H_1: \mu_i \neq \mu_j \text{ for at least one pair i, j}$$

Example: We test four types of mixing blades to determine the length of mixing times to achieve a homogeneous blend. The results for each treatment (blade type) appear in table 10.2. Perform a one-way Analysis of Variance test and determine if a significant difference exists at the α risk level of 0.05.

A note about α risk may be in order here. If the risk is set at 0.05, the result will not be rejected if the probability of F = 0.051, while it would be rejected if the probability of F = 0.049. It is important to calculate the probability of the test statistic beyond acceptance or rejection at a given level of α.

	Blade 1	Blade 2	Blade 3	Blade 4
	23.2	18.6	27.1	29.1
	26.7	24.7	22.2	22.8
	32.9	30.8	30.8	32.4
	23.6	20.2	19.5	20.9
	22.8		26.4	25.0
$Y_{.j}$	129.2	94.3	126	130.2
n	5	4	5	5
$y_{.j}^2$	16692.64	8892.49	15876.00	16952.04

Y.. = 129.2 + 94.3 + 126 + 130.2 = 479.7

$Y_{..}^2$ = 230,112.09

Table 10.2

Using equation (10-1), we find the treatment sum of squares:

$$SST = \frac{16692.64}{5} + \frac{8892.49}{4} + \frac{15876}{5} + \frac{16952.04}{5} - \frac{230,112.09}{19}$$

$$= 3338.53 + 2223.12 + 3175.20 + 3390.41 - 12,111.16 = 16.10$$

We find the total sum of squares using equation (10-2):

$$TSS = (23.2)^2 + (26.7)^2 + (32.9)^2 + (22.8)^2 + (18.6)^2 + \ldots +$$

$$(25.0)^2 - \frac{230,112.09}{19} = 12454.39 - 12,111.16 = 343.23$$

To calculate the sum of squares for error, we use equation (10-3):

$$SSE = 343.23 - 16.10 = 327.13$$

Then we place these values in the ANOVA table, which is table 10.3.

Source	Sum of Squares	Degrees of Freedom	Mean Square	F	Prob. > F
Between Treatments	16.10	3	5.36	0.246	0.86
Error	327.13	15	21.81		
Total	343.23	18			

Table 10.3

The F value for 3 and 15 degrees of freedom is 3.287. As the F calculated value of 0.246 < 3.287, do not reject H_0. The probability of an F value as large as 0.246 is 0.86, which is greater than the α level of 0.05, which again results in the acceptance of the null hypothesis. As a result, we do not reject the null hypothesis and conclude that there is not enough evidence to indicate any difference in mixing time between the four blade designs.

10.3 TWO-WAY ANOVA — FIXED EFFECTS MODEL, SINGLE REPLICATE

When a second factor is added to an experiment, or an experiment is blocked to remove the effects of extraneous factors, the result is a two-way model. The one-way model previously discussed had a single factor where each treatment level was replicated n times. With the addition of the second factor, the additional treatment levels will be designated as b. For example, if the second factor has five treatment (or blocking) levels, $b = 5$.

In this model we will only review a single replicate at each combination of levels, so $n = 1$ replicate. In the next section, we will discuss the $n > 1$ replicates.

For the two-way model, we will need additional equations. We will designate the second factor as blocks (B) to avoid confusion; this does not necessarily mean it was a blocking factor. Later we will discuss the effects of blocking.

When performing a two-way ANOVA, the a treatment levels will each be run the same number of times as there are blocking levels and the b blocking levels will each be run the same number of times as there are treatment levels.

The equation for the sum of squares of blocks is:

$$SSB = \sum_{i=1}^{b} \frac{y_{i.}^2}{a} - \frac{Y_{..}^2}{N} \qquad (10\text{-}4)$$

Where: $Y_{i.}$ = the sum of the ith row

The sum of squares for error is therefore:

$$SSE = TSS - SST - SSB \qquad (10\text{-}5)$$

which is similar to equation (10-3), with the additional value of SSB subtracted.

The ANOVA table for the two-way model appears in table 10.4.

Two-Way ANOVA Table					
Source	Sum of Squares	Degrees of Freedom	Mean Square	F	Prob. $>$ F
Treatments	SST	a - 1	$\frac{SST}{a\text{-}1}$	$\frac{MST}{MSE}$	
Blocks	SSB	b - 1	$\frac{SSB}{b\text{-}1}$	$\frac{MSB^*}{MSE}$	
Error	SSE	(a-1) (b-1)	$\frac{SSE}{(a\text{-}1)\,(b\text{-}1)}$	—	
Totals	TSS	N - 1			

Table 10.4

Note: If the purpose of the addition of the second factor is to block out systematic noise from the experiment, an F value and F test are deleted from the experiment. The experimenter assumes there is a significant difference in the blocks, which was the purpose of the blocking.

Example: We test four types of fuselage materials to determine any differences in their bonding strength. The adhesive, once mixed, is only workable long enough to allow four assemblies to be bonded together. This makes it necessary to mix a new batch of adhesive to bond the four assemblies together.

To block out any variations due to differences in the batches of adhesives, each of the four materials will be bonded from each batch of adhesive. The adhesive (block) sum of squares will then be removed from the overall sum of squares when performing the F test. The α level of risk for this test will be 0.05.

For this experiment, we will use five batches of adhesive. The number of treatments $a = 4$, and the number of blocks $b = 5$. The data from the experiment appears in table 10.5.

Adhesive Mixture	Material Type				Σy_i	Σy_i^2	a
	1	2	3	4			
1	21.9	20.3	20.5	20.5	83.2	6922.24	4
2	21.7	20.6	20.6	20.4	83.3	6938.89	4
3	21.2	20.7	21.0	20.7	83.6	6988.96	4
4	21.3	20.7	21.1	21.2	84.3	7106.49	4
5	21.8	20.9	20.6	20.6	83.9	7039.21	4
$Y_{.j}$	107.9	103.2	103.8	103.4	$\Sigma y_{i.} = 418.3$		
$Y_{.j}^2$	11642.41	10650.24	10774.44	10691.56	$\Sigma y_{i.}^2 = 34{,}995.79$		
b	5	5	5	5	$Y_{..} = 418.3$		
					$Y_{..}^2 = 179{,}974.89$		

Table 10.5

From equation (10-1) the treatment sum of squares is:

$$SST = \frac{11642.41 + 10650.24 + 10774.44 + 10691.56}{5} - \frac{174{,}974.89}{20}$$

$$SST = 2.986$$

From equation (10-3) the block sum of squares is:

$$SSB = \frac{6922.24 + 6938.89 + 6988.96 + 7106.49 + 7039.21}{4} - \frac{174,974.89}{20}$$

$$SSB = 0.203$$

From equation (10-2) the total sum of squares is:

$$TSS = (21.9)^2 + (21.7)^2 + \ldots + (20.6)^2 - \frac{174,974.89}{20}$$

$$TSS = 4.246$$

and from equation (10-5) the error sum of squares is:

$$SSE = 4.246 - 0.203 - 2.986 = 1.057$$

The next step is to construct the ANOVA table that is shown in table 10.6.

Two-Way ANOVA Table					
Source	Sum of Squares	Degrees of Freedom	Mean Square	F	Prob. > F
Treatments	2.986	3	0.995	11.31	0.0008
Blocks	0.203	4	0.051	—	—
Error	1.057	12	0.088	—	—
Total	4.246	19			

Table 10.6

Since the adhesive mixture was a blocking factor, an F test is not performed and is only used to remove noise from the experiment.

For $\alpha = 0.05$ and 3 and 12 degrees of freedom, the F value is 3.490. As the calculated value of F is larger than the table value, we reject the null hypothesis that all means are equal at $\alpha = 0.05$. As is evident on the right side of table 10.6, the probability of an F value as large as 11.31 for these degrees of freedom is only 0.0008, which is significantly less than the level set at 0.05.

10.4 TWO-WAY ANOVA — FIXED EFFECTS MODEL WITH REPLICATION

One of the assumptions in the previous two-way model is the absence of any interaction between the two factors or the main factor and blocking factor.

If we suspect that an interaction may exist, we must replicate each treatment combination experiment more than once to get an estimate of the interaction effect as well as the error.

The ANOVA table adapted from Montgomery appears in table 10.7, and model design appears in figure 10.1

Source	Sum of Squares	Degrees of Freedom	Mean Square	F	Prob. > F
A Treatments	SSA	a - 1	$\dfrac{SSA}{a-1}$	$\dfrac{MSA}{MSE}$	
B Treatments	SSB	b - 1	$\dfrac{SSB}{b-1}$	$\dfrac{MSB}{MSE}$	
Interaction	SSAxB	(a-1) (b-1)	$\dfrac{SSAxB}{(a-1)(b-1)}$	$\dfrac{SSAxB}{MSE}$	
Error	SSE	ab (n-1)	$\dfrac{SSE}{ab(n-1)}$		
Total	TSS	abn-1			

Table 10.7

Where: a = number of levels for factor A

b = number of levels for factor B

n = number of replicates

k = the kth replicate in row a, column b

Factor A					
		1	**2**	**.**	**.**	**b**

		1	2	.	.	b
F a c t o r **B**	**1**	y_{111}, y_{112} $\cdots, y_{11n}$	y_{121}, y_{122} $\cdots, y_{12n}$			y_{1b1}, y_{1b2} $\cdots, y_{1bn}$
	2	y_{211}, y_{212} $\cdots, y_{21n}$	y_{221}, y_{222} $\cdots, y_{22n}$			y_{2b1}, y_{2b2} $\cdots, y_{2bn}$
	.					
	.					
	a	y_{a11}, y_{a12} $\cdots, y_{a1n}$	y_{a21}, y_{a22} $\cdots, y_{a2n}$			y_{ab1}, y_{ab2} $\cdots, y_{abn}$

Figure 10.1

y_{111} = the first replicate in row 1, column 1

y_{112} = the second replicate in row 1, column 1

y_{11n} = the nth replicate in row 1, column 1

y_{abn} = the nth replicate in row a, column b

The equation for the total sum of squares for this model is:

$$TSS = \sum_{i=1}^{a} \sum_{j=1}^{b} \sum_{k=1}^{n} y_{ijk}^2 - \frac{Y...^2}{abn} \tag{10-6}$$

The sum of squares for factor A is calculated as:

$$SSA = \sum_{i=1}^{a} \frac{y_{i..}^2}{bn} - \frac{Y..^2}{abn} \tag{10-7}$$

The sum of squares for factor B is:

$$SSB = \sum_{i=1}^{b} \frac{y_{.j.}^2}{an} - \frac{Y...^2}{abn} \tag{10-8}$$

The interaction sum of squares is calculated as:

$$SSAxB = \sum_{i=1}^{a} \sum_{j=1}^{b} \frac{y_{ij.}^2}{n} - \sum_{i=1}^{a} \frac{y_{i..}^2}{bn} - \sum_{i=1}^{b} \frac{y_{.j.}^2}{an} + \frac{Y_{...}^2}{abn} \qquad (10\text{-}9)$$

and from the above equation, we calculate SSE as:

$$SSE = TSS - SSAxB - SSA - SSB \qquad (10\text{-}10)$$

Example: To improve the mileage on the line of large luxury cars, the manufacturer will test competing designs for both intake and exhaust manifolds. Four intake designs and three exhaust designs will be tested. Each combination will be replicated three times. Test for a significant difference in the designs at the 5% level of risk ($\alpha = 0.05$). The response variable will be miles per gallon.

The results of the experiment appear in figure 10.2.

For this example we have:

Factor A (intake) at four levels
Factor B (exhaust) at three levels
$n = 3$ (replicates)

Intake Designs									
			1		**2**		**3**		**4**
E x h a u s t	D e s i g n s	1	21 27 24	72	20 27 29	76	31 30 36	97	24 24 25	73
		2	26 24 22	72	25 21 26	72	34 37 34	105	28 21 26	75
		3	25 24 29	78	22 28 23	73	31 35 33	99	26 25 29	80

Figure 10.2

The boxed values in figure 10.2 are the cell totals.

From equation (10-6) the total sum of squares is:

$$TSS = 26966 - \frac{972^2}{36} = 722$$

From equation (10-7) SSA is:

$$\text{SS Intake} = 26745.56 - 26244 = 501.56$$

From equation (10-8) SSB is:

$$\text{SS Exhaust} = 26250 - 26244 = 6.000$$

From equation (10-9) the Intake x Exhaust interaction sum of squares SSAxB is:

$$\text{SS Intake x Exhaust} = 26776.67 - 26745.56 - 26250 + 26244 = 25.11$$

and from equation (10-10) the error sum of squares is:

$$\text{SSE} = 722 - 501.56 - 6 - 25.11 = 189.33$$

We then place the previously calculated sums of squares and degrees of freedom in the ANOVA table, as shown in table 10.8

Source	Sum of Squares	Degrees of Freedom	Mean Square	F	Prob. > F
Intake (A)	501.56	3	167.19	21.19	0.0000
Exhaust (B)	6.00	2	3.00	0.38	0.688
Intake x Exhaust Interaction (AxB)	25.11	6	4.19	0.53	0.780
Error	189.33	24	7.89		
Total	722	35			

Table 10.8

The F value for Intake of 21.19 is compared to F table value for $\alpha = 0.05$ and 3 and 24 df, which is 3.01. The calculated value of F exceeds this value, so we reject the null hypothesis of all means being equal at the α risk level of 0.05. The actual probability is about zero. There is a significant difference in the means of the intake manifolds.

The probability values for exhaust (2 and 24 df) and interacton (6 and 24 df) are 0.688 and 0.78, respectively. Since these probabilities are greater than the risk value of 0.05, we do not reject the null hypotheses, and we conclude there is no significant difference between exhaust manifolds, nor is there significant interaction effect.

10.5 RANDOM EFFECTS MODEL

In previous sections, all models were fixed effects models. In section 10.4 the intake manifold design was fixed at four levels, and in section 10.2 the blades were fixed at four levels. In each case, we tested all the levels of every factor available for testing. No extrapolation beyond the levels tested is made or intended.

There are times when there are too many levels to test every level and we draw a random sample to perform the analysis. This is the random effects model, sometimes referred to as the components of variance model. It determines the amount of variation due to the factor, compared to the total variation present in the system.

When performing an analysis on a random effects model, the statistical analysis and ANOVA table and tests are the same as in the fixed effects model. If the F test shows that a significant difference exists, the factor can be broken down into its components of variance for analysis.

The components of variance for a given factor are developed from the relationship of:

$$\frac{\text{MS Factor A}}{\text{MSE}} = \frac{\sigma^2_{\text{ERROR}} + n\sigma^2_A}{\sigma^2_{\text{ERROR}}} \tag{10-11}$$

For example, in the example used in section 10.3, only the material type was under consideration, and when tested, it proved significant at the level of risk given. This was in a sense a single factor experiment at four treatment levels (a = 4) replicated five times (n = 5).

The first step in isolating the variation is to manipulate equation (10-11) to achieve:

$$\sigma^2_A = \frac{\text{MSA} - \text{MSE}}{n} \tag{10-12}$$

and the total variation in the system is given by:

$$\sigma^2_{\text{SYSTEM}} = \sigma^2_{\text{ERROR}} + \sigma^2_A \tag{10-13}$$

Where: σ^2_{SYSTEM} = total variation in the system

σ^2_{ERROR} = residual error

σ^2_A = variation effect of the factor

The variation due to the factor is then compared to the total variation in the system and multiplied by 100 for a percentage.

$$\text{Factor variation} = \frac{\sigma^2_A}{\sigma^2_{\text{SYSTEM}}} \times 100 \tag{10-14}$$

Example: Using the example from section 10.3, estimate the amount of variation in the system caused by material types, if the four levels chosen are a random sample from several possible levels.

The residual error σ^2_{ERROR} is provided by the value for MSE, which is 0.088. The mean square for the factor is given as MSA, which is SST/a-1 = 0.995.

Manipulating the fact that MSA = SST/a-1, and that this estimate of MSA also contains residual error, we find that from equation (10-11):

$$0.995 = 0.088 + 5\sigma^2_A$$

and from equation (10-12):

$$\sigma^2_A = \frac{0.995 - 0.088}{5} = 0.181$$

The variation in the total system is given by equation (10-13):

$$\sigma^2_{SYSTEM} = 0.088 + 0.181 = 0.269$$

The amount of variation as a result of material types to the total system is given by equation (10-14):

$$\frac{0.181}{0.269} \times 100 = 67.29\%$$

Thus, material types result in about 67% of the total variation in the system.

OTHER MODELS

There are other models not covered, including mixed models, which are a combination of fixed and random factors. For further discussion, see the text by Hicks.

11.0 TABLES

TABLE A

Normal Distribution

AREA FROM MEAN TO Z

Z	.00	.01	.02	.03	.04	.05	.06	.07	.08	.09
0.0	0.0000	.0040	.0080	.0120	.0160	.0199	.0239	.0279	.0319	.0359
.1	.0398	.0438	.0478	.0517	.0557	.0596	.0636	.0675	.0714	.0753
.2	.0793	.0832	.0871	.0910	.0948	.0987	.1026	.1064	.1103	.1141
.3	.1179	.1217	.1255	.1293	.1331	.1368	.1406	.1443	.1480	.1517
.4	.1554	.1591	.1628	.1664	.1700	.1736	.1772	.1808	.1844	.1879
.5	.1915	.1950	.1985	.2019	.2054	.2088	.2123	.2157	.2190	.2224
.6	.2257	.2291	.1324	.2357	.2389	.2422	.2454	.2486	.2517	.2549
.7	.2580	.2611	.2642	.2673	.2704	.2734	.2764	.2794	.2823	.2852
.8	.2881	.2910	.2939	.2967	.2995	.3023	.3051	.3078	.3106	.3133
.9	.3159	.3186	.3212	.3238	.3264	.3289	.3315	.3340	.3365	.3389
1.0	.3413	.3438	.3461	.3485	.3508	.3531	.3554	.3577	.3599	.3621
1.1	.3643	.3665	.3686	.3708	.3729	.3749	.3770	.3790	.3810	.3830
1.2	.3849	.3869	.3888	.3907	.3925	.3944	.3962	.3980	.3997	.4015
1.3	.4032	.4049	.4066	.4082	.4099	.4115	.4131	.4147	.4162	.4177
1.4	.4192	.4207	.4222	.4236	.4251	.4265	.4279	.4292	.4306	.4319
1.5	.4332	.4345	.4357	.4370	.4382	.4394	.4406	.4418	.4429	.4441
1.6	.4452	.4463	.4474	.4484	.4495	.4505	.4515	.4525	.4535	.4545
1.7	.4554	.4564	.4573	.4582	.4591	.4599	.4608	.4616	.4625	.4633
1.8	.4641	.4649	.4656	.4664	.4671	.4678	.4686	.4693	.4699	.4706
1.9	.4713	.4719	.4726	.4732	.4738	.4744	.4750	.4756	.4761	.4767
2.0	.4772	.4778	.4783	.4788	.4793	.4798	.4803	.4808	.4812	.4817
2.1	.4821	.4826	.4830	.4834	.4838	.4842	.4846	.4850	.4854	.4857
2.2	.4861	.4864	.4868	.4871	.4875	.4878	.4881	.4884	.4887	.4890
2.3	.4893	.4896	.4898	.4901	.4904	.4906	.4909	.4911	.4913	.4916
2.4	.4918	.4920	.4922	.4925	.4927	.4929	.4931	.4932	.4934	.4936
2.5	.4938	.4940	.4941	.4943	.4945	.4946	.4948	.4949	.4951	.4952
2.6	.4953	.4955	.4956	.4957	.4959	.4960	.4961	.4962	.4963	.4964
2.7	.4965	.4966	.4967	.4968	.4969	.4970	.4971	.4972	.4973	.4974
2.8	.4974	.4975	.4976	.4977	.4977	.4978	.4979	.4979	.4980	.4981
2.9	.4981	.4982	.4982	.4983	.4984	.4984	.4985	.4985	.4986	.4986
3.0	.4987	.4987	.4987	.4988	.4988	.4989	.4989	.4989	.4990	.4990

TABLE A (cont.)

AREA BELOW Z

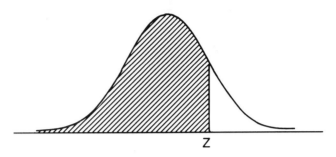

Z

Z	.00	.01	.02	.03	.04	.05	.06	.07	.08	.09
0.0	.5000	.5040	.5080	.5120	.5160	.5199	.5239	.5279	.5319	.5359
.1	.5398	.5438	.5478	.5517	.5557	.5596	.5636	.5674	.5714	.5753
.2	.5793	.5832	.5871	.5910	.5948	.5987	.6026	.6064	.6103	.6141
.3	.6179	.6217	.6255	.6293	.6331	.6368	.6406	.6443	.6480	.6517
.4	.6554	.6519	.6628	.6664	.6700	.6736	.6772	.6808	.6844	.6879
.5	.6915	.6950	.6985	.7019	.7054	.7088	.7123	.7157	.7190	.7224
.6	.7257	.7291	.7324	.7357	.7389	.7422	.7454	.7486	.7517	.7549
.7	.7580	.7611	.7642	.7673	.7704	.7734	.7764	.7794	.7823	.7852
.8	.7881	.7910	.7939	.7967	.7995	.8023	.8051	.8078	.8106	.8133
.9	.8159	.8186	.8212	.8238	.8264	.8289	.8315	.8340	.8365	.8389
1.0	.8413	.8438	.8461	.8485	.8508	.8531	.8554	.8577	.8599	.8621
1.1	.8643	.8665	.8686	.8708	.8729	.8749	.8770	.8790	.8810	.8830
1.2	.8849	.8869	.8888	.8907	.8925	.8944	.8962	.8980	.8997	.9015
1.3	.9032	.9049	.9066	.9082	.9099	.9115	.9131	.9147	.9162	.9177
1.4	.9192	.9207	.9222	.9236	.9251	.9265	.9279	.9292	.9306	.9319
1.5	.9332	.9345	.9357	.9370	.9382	.9394	.9406	.9418	.9429	.9441
1.6	.9452	.9463	.9474	.9484	.9495	.9505	.9515	.9525	.9535	.9545
1.7	.9554	.9564	.9573	.9582	.9591	.9599	.9608	.9616	.9625	.9633
1.8	.9641	.9649	.9656	.9664	.9671	.9678	.9686	.9693	.9699	.9706
1.9	.9713	.9719	.9726	.9732	.9738	.9744	.9750	.9756	.9761	.9767
2.0	.9772	.9778	.9783	.9788	.9793	.9798	.9803	.9808	.9812	.9817
2.1	.9821	.9826	.9830	.9834	.9838	.9842	.9846	.9850	.9954	.9857
2.2	.9861	.9864	.9868	.9871	.9875	.9878	.9881	.9884	.9887	.9890
2.3	.9893	.9896	.9898	.9901	.9904	.9906	.9909	.9911	.9913	.9916
2.4	.9918	.9920	.9922	.9925	.9927	.9929	.9931	.9932	.9934	.9936
2.5	.9938	.9940	.9941	.9943	.9945	.9946	.9948	.9949	.9951	.9952
2.6	.9953	.9955	.9956	.9957	.9959	.9960	.9961	.9962	.9963	.9964
2.7	.9965	.9966	.9967	.9968	.9969	.9970	.9971	.9972	.9973	.9974
2.8	.9974	.9975	.9976	.9977	.9977	.9978	.9979	.9979	.9980	.9981
2.9	.9981	.9982	.9982	.9983	.9984	.9984	.9985	.9985	.9986	.9986
3.0	.9987	.9987	.9987	.9988	.9988	.9989	.9989	.9989	.9990	.9990

TABLE A (cont.)

Normal Distribution

AREA BEYOND Z

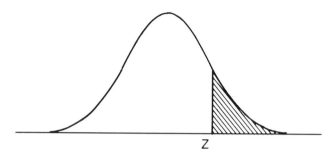

Z

Z	.00	.01	.02	.03	.04	.05	.06	.07	.08	.09
0.0	.5000	.4960	.4920	.4880	.4840	.4801	.4761	.4721	.4681	.4641
.1	.4602	.4562	.4522	.4483	.4443	.4404	.4364	.4325	.4286	.4247
.2	.4207	.4168	.4129	.4090	.4052	.4013	.3974	.3936	.3897	.3859
.3	.3821	.3783	.3745	.3707	.3669	.3632	.3594	.3557	.3520	.3483
.4	.3446	.3481	.3372	.3336	.3300	.3264	.3228	.3192	.3156	.3121
.5	.3085	.3050	.3015	.2981	.2946	.2912	.2877	.2843	.2810	.2776
.6	.2743	.2709	.2676	.2643	.2611	.2578	.2546	.2514	.2483	.2451
.7	.2420	.2389	.2358	.2327	.2296	.2266	.2236	.2206	.2177	.2148
.8	.2119	.2090	.2061	.2033	.2005	.1977	.1949	.1922	.1894	.1867
.9	.1841	.1814	.1788	.1762	.1736	.1711	.1685	.1660	.1635	.1611
1.0	.1587	.1562	.1539	.1515	.1492	.1469	.1446	.1423	.1401	.1379
1.1	.1357	.1335	.1314	.1292	.1271	.1251	.1230	.1210	.1190	.1170
1.2	.1151	.1131	.1112	.1093	.1075	.1056	.1038	.1020	.1003	.0985
1.3	.0968	.0951	.0934	.0918	.0901	.0885	.0869	.0853	.0838	.0823
1.4	.0808	.0793	.0778	.0764	.0749	.0735	.0721	.0708	.0694	.0681
1.5	.0668	.0655	.0643	.0630	.0618	.0606	.0594	.0582	.0571	.0559
1.6	.0548	.0537	.0526	.0516	.0505	.0495	.0485	.0475	.0465	.0455
1.7	.0446	.0436	.0427	.0418	.0409	.0401	.0392	.0384	.0375	.0367
1.8	.0359	.0351	.0344	.0336	.0329	.0322	.0314	.0307	.0301	.0294
1.9	.0287	.0281	.0274	.0268	.0262	.0256	.0250	.0244	.0239	.0233
2.0	.0228	.0222	.0217	.0212	.0207	.0202	.0197	.0192	.0188	.0183
2.1	.0179	.0174	.0170	.0166	.0162	.0158	.0154	.0150	.0146	.0143
2.2	.0139	.0136	.0132	.0129	.0125	.0122	.0119	.0116	.0113	.0110
2.3	.0107	.0104	.0102	.0099	.0096	.0094	.0091	.0089	.0087	.0084
2.4	.0082	.0080	.0078	.0075	.0073	.0071	.0069	.0068	.0066	.0064
2.5	.0062	.0060	.0059	.0057	.0055	.0054	.0052	.0051	.0049	.0048
2.6	.0047	.0045	.0044	.0043	.0041	.0040	.0039	.0038	.0037	.0036
2.7	.0035	.0034	.0033	.0032	.0031	.0030	.0029	.0028	.0027	.0026
2.8	.0026	.0025	.0024	.0023	.0023	.0022	.0021	.0021	.0020	.0019
2.9	.0019	.0018	.0018	.0017	.0016	.0016	.0015	.0015	.0014	.0014
3.0	.0013	.0013	.0013	.0012	.0012	.0011	.0011	.0011	.0010	.0010

TABLE B

Percentage Points, Students' *t* Distribution
(Upper-tail probabilities)

ν \ α	0.40	0.25	0.10	0.05	0.025	0.01	0.005	0.0005
1	0.325	1.000	3.078	6.314	12.706	31.821	63.657	636.619
2	0.289	0.816	1.886	2.920	4.303	6.965	9.925	31.598
3	0.277	0.765	1.638	2.353	3.182	4.541	5.841	12.941
4	0.271	0.741	1.533	2.132	2.776	3.747	4.604	8.610
5	0.267	0.727	1.476	2.015	2.571	3.365	4.032	6.859
6	0.265	0.718	1.440	1.943	2.447	3.143	3.707	5.959
7	0.263	0.711	1.415	1.895	2.365	2.998	3.499	5.405
8	0.262	0.706	1.397	1.860	2.306	2.896	3.355	5.041
9	0.261	0.703	1.383	1.833	2.262	2.821	3.250	4.781
10	0.260	0.700	1.372	1.812	2.228	2.764	3.169	4.587
11	0.260	0.697	1.363	1.796	2.201	2.718	3.106	4.437
12	0.259	0.695	1.356	1.782	2.179	2.681	3.055	4.318
13	0.259	0.694	1.350	1.771	2.160	2.650	3.012	4.221
14	0.258	0.692	1.345	1.761	2.145	2.624	2.977	4.140
15	0.258	0.691	1.341	1.753	2.131	2.602	2.947	4.073
16	0.258	0.690	1.337	1.746	2.120	2.583	2.921	4.015
17	0.257	0.689	1.333	1.740	2.110	2.567	2.898	3.965
18	0.257	0.688	1.330	1.734	2.101	2.552	2.878	3.922
19	0.257	0.688	1.328	1.729	2.093	2.539	2.861	3.883
20	0.257	0.687	1.325	1.725	2.086	2.528	2.845	3.850
21	0.257	0.686	1.323	1.721	2.080	2.518	2.831	3.819
22	0.256	0.686	1.321	1.717	2.074	2.508	2.819	3.792
23	0.256	0.685	1.319	1.714	2.069	2.500	2.807	3.767
24	0.256	0.687	1.318	1.711	2.064	2.492	2.797	3.745
25	0.256	0.684	1.316	1.708	2.060	2.485	2.787	3.725
26	0.256	0.684	1.315	1.706	2.056	2.479	2.779	3.707
27	0.256	0.684	1.314	1.703	2.052	2.473	2.771	3.690
28	0.256	0.683	1.313	1.701	2.048	2.467	2.763	3.674
29	0.256	0.683	1.311	1.699	2.045	2.462	2.756	3.659
30	0.256	0.683	1.310	1.697	2.042	2.457	2.750	3.656
40	0.255	0.681	1.303	1.684	2.021	2.423	2.704	3.551
60	0.254	0.679	1.296	1.671	2.000	2.390	2.660	3.460
120	0.254	0.677	1.289	1.658	1.980	2.358	2.617	3.373
∞	0.253	0.674	1.282	1.645	1.960	2.326	2.576	3.291
ν \ 2α	0.80	0.50	0.20	0.10	0.05	0.02	0.01	0.001

(Two-tail probabilities)

SOURCE: Table 2 is taken from Table III of Fisher and Yates: *Statistical Tables for Biological, Agricultural and Medical Research,* published by Longman Group Ltd., London (previously published by Oliver & Boyd, Edinburgh), and by permission of the authors and publishers.

TABLE C

Distribution of Chi-Square

df	0.99	0.98	0.95	0.90	0.80	0.70	0.50	0.30	0.20	0.10	0.05	0.02	0.01	0.001
1	0.0157	0.0628	0.00393	0.0158	0.0642	0.148	0.455	1.074	1.642	2.706	3.841	5.412	6.635	10.827
2	0.0201	0.0404	0.103	0.211	0.446	0.713	1.386	2.408	3.219	4.605	5.991	7.824	9.210	13.815
3	0.115	0.185	0.352	0.584	1.005	1.424	2.366	3.665	4.642	6.251	7.815	9.837	11.341	16.268
4	0.297	0.429	0.711	1.064	1.649	2.195	3.357	4.878	5.989	7.779	9.488	11.668	13.277	18.465
5	0.554	0.752	1.145	1.610	2.343	3.000	4.351	6.064	7.289	9.236	11.070	13.388	15.086	20.517
6	0.872	1.134	1.635	2.204	3.070	3.828	5.348	7.231	8.558	10.645	12.592	15.033	16.812	22.457
7	1.239	1.564	2.167	2.833	3.822	4.671	6.346	8.383	9.803	12.017	14.067	16.622	18.475	24.322
8	1.646	2.032	2.733	3.490	4.594	5.527	7.344	9.524	11.030	13.362	15.507	18.168	20.090	26.125
9	2.088	2.532	3.325	4.168	5.380	6.393	8.343	10.656	12.242	14.684	16.919	19.679	21.666	27.877
10	2.558	3.059	3.940	4.865	6.179	7.267	9.342	11.781	13.442	15.987	18.307	21.161	23.209	29.588
11	3.053	3.609	4.575	5.578	6.989	8.148	10.341	12.899	14.631	17.275	19.675	22.618	24.725	31.264
12	3.571	4.178	5.226	6.304	7.807	9.034	11.340	14.011	15.812	18.549	21.026	24.054	26.217	32.909
13	4.107	4.765	5.892	7.042	8.634	9.926	12.340	15.119	16.985	19.812	22.362	25.472	27.688	34.528
14	4.660	5.368	6.571	7.790	9.467	10.821	13.339	16.222	18.151	21.064	23.685	26.873	29.141	36.123
15	5.229	5.985	7.261	8.547	10.307	11.721	14.339	17.322	19.311	22.307	24.996	28.259	30.578	37.697
16	5.812	6.614	7.962	9.312	11.152	12.624	15.338	18.418	20.465	23.542	26.296	29.663	32.000	39.252
17	6.408	7.255	8.762	10.085	12.002	13.531	16.338	19.511	21.615	24.769	27.587	30.995	33.409	40.790
18	7.015	7.906	9.390	10.865	12.857	14.440	17.338	20.601	22.760	25.989	28.869	32.346	34.805	42.312
19	7.633	8.567	10.117	11.651	13.716	15.352	18.338	21.689	23.900	27.204	30.144	33.687	36.191	43.820
20	8.260	9.237	10.851	12.443	14.578	16.266	19.337	22.775	25.038	28.412	31.410	35.020	37.566	45.315
21	8.897	9.915	11.591	13.240	15.445	17.182	20.337	23.858	26.171	29.615	32.671	36.343	38.932	46.797
22	9.542	10.600	12.338	14.041	16.314	18.101	21.337	24.939	27.301	30.813	33.924	37.659	40.289	48.268
23	10.196	11.293	13.091	14.848	17.187	19.021	22.337	26.018	28.429	32.007	35.172	38.968	41.638	49.728
24	10.856	11.992	13.848	15.659	18.062	19.943	23.337	27.096	29.553	33.196	36.415	40.270	42.980	51.179
25	11.524	12.697	14.611	16.473	18.940	20.867	24.337	28.172	30.675	34.382	37.652	41.566	44.314	52.620
26	12.198	13.409	15.379	17.292	19.820	21.792	25.336	29.246	31.795	35.563	38.885	42.856	45.642	54.052
27	12.879	14.125	16.151	18.114	20.703	22.719	26.336	30.319	32.912	36.741	40.113	44.140	46.963	55.476
28	13.565	14.847	16.928	18.939	21.588	23.647	27.336	31.391	34.027	37.916	41.337	45.419	48.278	56.893
29	14.256	15.574	17.708	19.768	22.475	24.577	28.336	32.461	35.139	39.087	42.557	46.693	49.588	58.302
30	14.953	16.306	18.493	20.599	23.364	25.508	29.336	33.530	36.250	40.256	43.773	47.962	50.892	59.703

Reprinted with permission of ASQC Quality Press.

TABLE D

Percentages of the F Distribution - $\alpha = 0.05$
$\alpha = 0.05$ (upper-tail)

ν_2 \ ν_1	1	2	3	4	5	6	7	8	9
1	161.4	199.5	215.7	224.6	230.2	234.0	236.8	238.9	240.5
2	18.51	19.00	19.16	19.25	19.30	19.33	19.35	19.37	19.38
3	10.13	9.55	9.28	9.12	9.01	8.94	8.89	8.85	8.81
4	7.71	6.94	6.59	6.39	6.26	6.16	6.08	6.04	6.00
5	6.61	5.79	5.41	5.19	5.05	4.95	4.88	4.82	4.77
6	5.99	5.14	4.76	4.53	4.39	4.28	4.21	4.15	4.10
7	5.59	4.74	4.35	4.12	3.97	3.87	3.79	3.73	3.68
8	5.32	4.46	4.07	3.84	3.69	3.58	3.50	3.44	3.39
9	5.12	4.26	3.86	3.63	3.48	3.37	3.29	3.23	3.18
10	4.96	4.10	3.71	3.48	3.33	3.22	3.14	3.07	3.02
11	4.84	3.98	3.59	3.36	3.20	3.09	3.01	2.95	2.90
12	4.75	3.89	3.49	3.26	3.11	3.00	2.91	2.85	2.80
13	4.67	3.81	3.41	3.18	3.03	2.92	2.83	2.77	2.71
14	4.60	3.74	3.34	3.11	2.96	2.85	2.76	2.70	2.65
15	4.54	3.68	3.29	3.06	2.90	2.79	2.71	2.64	2.59
16	4.49	3.63	3.24	3.01	2.85	2.74	2.66	2.59	2.54
17	4.45	3.59	3.20	2.96	2.81	2.70	2.61	2.55	2.49
18	4.41	3.55	3.16	2.93	2.77	2.66	2.58	2.51	2.46
19	4.38	3.52	3.13	2.90	3.74	2.63	2.54	2.48	2.42
20	4.35	3.49	3.10	2.87	2.71	2.60	2.51	2.45	2.39
21	4.32	3.47	3.07	2.84	2.68	2.57	2.49	2.42	2.37
22	4.30	3.44	3.05	2.82	2.66	2.55	2.46	2.40	2.34
23	4.28	3.42	3.03	2.80	2.64	2.53	2.44	2.37	2.32
24	4.26	3.40	3.01	2.78	2.62	2.51	2.42	2.36	2.30
25	4.24	3.39	2.99	2.76	2.60	2.49	2.40	2.34	2.28
26	4.23	3.37	2.98	2.74	2.59	2.47	2.39	2.32	2.27
27	4.21	3.35	2.96	2.73	2.57	2.46	2.37	2.31	2.25
28	4.20	3.34	2.95	2.71	2.56	2.45	2.36	2.29	2.24
29	4.18	3.33	2.93	2.70	2.55	2.43	2.35	2.28	2.22
30	4.17	3.32	2.92	2.69	2.53	2.42	2.33	2.27	2.21
40	4.08	3.23	2.84	2.61	2.45	2.34	2.25	2.18	2.12
60	4.00	3.15	2.76	2.53	2.37	2.25	2.17	2.10	2.04
120	3.92	3.07	2.68	2.45	2.29	2.17	2.09	2.02	1.96
∞	3.84	3.00	2.60	2.37	2.21	2.10	2.01	1.94	1.88

$F_{(\nu_1, \nu_2, 1-\alpha)} = 1/F_{(\nu_2, \nu_1, \alpha)}$

TABLE D (cont.)

Percentages of the F Distribution - α = 0.05

10	12	15	20	24	30	40	60	120	∞
241.9	243.9	245.9	248.0	249.1	250.1	251.1	252.2	253.3	254.3
19.40	19.41	19.43	19.45	19.45	19.46	19.47	19.48	19.49	19.50
8.79	8.74	8.70	8.68	8.64	8.62	8.59	8.57	8.55	8.53
5.96	5.91	5.86	5.80	5.77	5.75	5.72	5.69	5.66	5.63
4.74	4.68	4.62	4.56	4.53	4.50	4.46	4.43	4.40	4.36
4.06	4.00	3.94	3.87	3.84	3.81	3.77	3.74	3.70	3.67
3.64	3.57	3.51	3.44	3.41	3.38	3.34	3.30	3.27	3.23
3.35	3.28	3.22	3.15	3.12	3.08	3.04	3.01	2.97	2.93
3.14	3.07	3.01	2.94	2.90	2.86	2.83	2.79	2.75	2.71
2.98	2.91	2.85	2.77	2.74	2.70	2.66	2.62	2.58	2.54
2.85	2.79	2.72	2.65	2.61	2.57	2.53	2.49	2.45	2.40
2.75	2.69	2.62	2.54	2.51	2.47	2.43	2.38	2.34	2.30
2.67	2.60	2.53	2.46	2.42	2.38	2.34	2.30	2.25	2.21
2.60	2.53	2.46	2.39	2.35	2.31	2.27	2.22	2.18	2.13
2.54	2.48	2.40	2.33	2.29	2.25	2.20	2.16	2.11	2.07
2.49	2.42	2.35	2.28	2.24	2.19	2.15	2.11	2.06	2.01
2.45	2.38	2.31	2.23	2.19	2.15	2.10	2.06	2.01	1.96
2.41	2.34	2.27	2.19	2.15	2.11	2.06	2.02	1.97	1.92
2.38	2.31	2.23	2.16	2.11	2.07	2.03	1.98	1.93	1.88
2.35	2.28	2.20	2.12	2.08	2.04	1.99	1.95	1.90	1.84
2.32	2.25	2.18	2.10	2.05	2.01	1.95	1.92	1.87	1.81
2.30	2.23	2.15	2.07	2.03	1.98	1.94	1.89	1.84	1.78
2.27	2.20	2.13	2.05	2.01	1.96	1.91	1.86	1.81	1.76
2.25	2.18	2.11	2.03	1.98	1.94	1.89	1.84	1.79	1.73
2.24	2.16	2.09	2.01	1.96	1.92	1.87	1.82	1.77	1.71
2.22	2.15	2.07	1.99	1.95	1.90	1.85	1.80	1.75	1.69
2.20	2.13	2.06	1.97	1.93	1.88	1.84	1.79	1.73	1.67
2.19	2.12	2.04	1.96	1.91	1.87	1.82	1.77	1.71	1.65
2.18	2.10	2.03	1.94	1.90	1.85	1.81	1.75	1.70	1.64
2.16	2.09	2.01	1.93	1.89	1.84	1.79	1.74	1.68	1.62
2.08	2.00	1.92	1.84	1.79	1.74	1.69	1.64	1.58	1.51
1.99	1.92	1.84	1.75	1.70	1.65	1.59	1.53	1.47	1.39
1.91	1.83	1.75	1.66	1.61	1.55	1.50	1.43	1.35	1.25
1.83	1.75	1.67	1.57	1.52	1.46	1.39	1.32	1.22	1.00

Source: *Biometrika Tables for Statisticians*, 3d. Ed., University College, London, 1966.

TABLE D

Percentages of the F Distribution - α = 0.01
α = 0.01 (upper-tail)

ν_2 \ ν_1	1	2	3	4	5	6	7	8	9
1	4052	4999.5	5403	5625	5764	5859	5928	5982	6022
2	98.50	99.00	99.17	99.25	99.30	99.33	99.36	99.37	99.39
3	34.12	30.82	29.46	28.71	28.24	27.91	27.67	27.49	27.35
4	21.20	18.00	16.69	15.98	15.52	15.21	14.98	14.80	14.66
5	16.26	13.27	12.06	11.39	10.97	10.67	10.46	10.29	10.16
6	13.75	10.92	9.78	9.15	8.75	8.47	8.26	8.10	7.98
7	12.25	9.55	8.45	7.85	8.46	7.19	6.99	6.84	6.72
8	11.26	8.65	7.59	7.01	6.63	6.37	6.18	6.03	5.91
9	10.56	8.02	6.99	6.42	6.06	5.80	5.61	5.47	5.35
10	10.04	7.56	6.55	5.99	5.64	5.39	5.20	5.06	4.94
11	9.65	7.21	6.22	5.67	5.32	5.07	4.89	4.74	4.63
12	9.33	6.93	5.95	5.41	5.06	4.82	4.64	4.50	4.39
13	9.07	6.70	5.74	5.21	4.86	4.62	4.44	4.30	4.19
14	8.86	6.51	5.56	5.04	4.69	4.46	4.28	4.14	4.03
15	8.68	6.36	5.42	4.89	4.56	4.32	4.14	4.00	3.89
16	8.53	6.23	5.29	4.77	4.44	4.20	4.03	3.89	3.78
17	8.40	6.11	5.18	4.67	4.34	4.10	3.93	3.79	3.68
18	8.29	6.01	5.09	4.58	4.25	4.01	3.84	3.71	3.60
19	8.18	5.93	5.01	4.50	4.17	3.94	3.77	3.63	3.52
20	8.10	5.85	4.94	4.43	4.10	3.87	3.70	3.56	3.46
21	8.02	5.78	4.87	4.37	4.04	3.81	3.64	3.51	3.40
22	7.95	5.72	4.82	4.31	3.99	3.76	3.59	3.45	3.35
23	7.88	5.66	4.76	4.26	3.94	3.71	3.54	3.41	3.30
24	7.82	5.61	4.72	4.22	3.90	3.67	3.50	3.36	3.26
25	7.77	5.57	4.68	4.18	3.85	3.63	3.46	3.32	3.22
26	7.72	5.53	4.64	4.14	3.82	3.59	3.42	3.29	3.18
27	7.68	5.49	4.00	4.11	3.78	3.56	3.39	3.26	3.15
28	7.64	5.45	4.57	4.07	3.75	3.53	3.36	3.23	3.12
29	7.60	5.42	4.54	4.04	3.73	3.50	3.33	3.20	3.09
30	7.56	5.39	4.51	4.02	3.70	3.47	3.30	3.17	3.07
40	7.31	5.18	4.31	3.83	3.51	3.29	3.12	2.99	2.89
60	7.08	4.98	4.13	3.65	3.34	3.12	2.95	2.82	2.72
120	6.85	4.79	3.95	3.48	3.17	2.96	2.79	2.66	2.56
∞	6.63	4.61	3.78	3.32	3.02	2.80	2.64	2.51	2.41

$F_{(\nu_1, \nu_2, 1-\alpha)} = 1/F_{(\nu_2, \nu_1, \alpha)}$

TABLE D (cont.)

Percentages of the F Distribution - $\alpha = 0.01$

10	12	15	20	24	30	40	60	120	∞
6056	6106	6157	6209	6235	6261	6287	6313	6339	6366
99.40	99.42	99.43	99.45	99.46	99.47	99.47	99.48	99.49	99.50
27.23	27.05	26.87	26.69	26.60	26.50	26.41	26.32	26.22	26.13
14.55	14.37	14.20	14.02	13.93	13.81	13.75	13.65	13.56	13.46
10.05	9.89	9.72	9.55	9.47	9.38	9.29	9.20	9.11	9.02
7.87	7.72	7.53	7.40	7.31	7.23	7.14	7.06	6.97	6.88
6.62	6.47	6.31	6.16	6.07	5.99	5.91	5.82	5.74	5.65
5.81	5.67	5.52	5.35	5.28	5.20	5.12	5.03	4.95	4.86
5.26	5.11	4.96	4.81	4.73	4.65	4.57	4.48	4.40	4.31
4.85	4.71	4.56	4.41	4.33	4.25	4.17	4.08	4.00	3.91
4.54	4.40	4.25	4.10	4.02	3.94	3.86	3.78	3.69	3.60
4.30	4.16	4.01	3.83	3.78	3.70	3.62	3.54	3.45	3.36
4.10	3.96	3.82	3.66	3.59	3.51	3.43	3.34	3.25	3.17
3.94	3.80	3.66	3.51	3.43	3.35	3.27	3.18	3.09	3.00
3.80	3.67	3.52	3.37	3.29	3.21	3.13	3.05	2.96	2.87
3.69	3.55	3.41	3.26	3.18	3.10	3.02	2.93	2.84	2.75
3.59	3.46	3.31	3.16	3.08	3.00	2.92	2.83	2.75	2.65
3.51	3.37	3.23	3.03	3.00	2.92	2.84	2.75	2.66	2.57
3.43	3.30	3.15	3.00	2.92	2.84	2.70	2.67	2.58	2.49
3.37	3.23	3.09	2.94	2.86	2.78	2.69	2.61	2.52	2.42
3.31	3.17	3.03	2.88	2.80	2.72	2.64	2.55	2.46	2.36
3.26	3.12	2.98	2.83	2.75	2.67	2.58	2.50	2.40	2.31
3.21	3.07	2.93	2.78	2.70	2.62	2.54	2.45	2.35	2.26
3.17	3.03	2.89	2.74	2.66	2.58	2.49	2.40	2.31	2.21
3.13	2.99	2.85	2.70	2.62	2.54	2.45	2.36	2.27	2.17
3.09	2.96	2.81	2.66	2.58	2.50	2.42	2.33	2.23	2.13
3.06	2.93	2.78	2.63	2.55	2.47	2.38	2.29	2.20	2.10
3.03	2.90	2.75	2.60	2.52	2.44	2.35	2.26	2.17	2.06
3.00	2.87	2.73	2.57	2.49	2.41	2.33	2.23	2.14	2.03
2.93	2.84	2.70	2.55	2.47	2.39	2.30	2.21	2.11	2.01
2.80	2.63	2.52	2.37	2.29	2.20	2.11	2.02	1.92	1.80
2.63	2.50	2.35	2.20	2.12	2.03	1.94	1.84	1.73	1.60
2.47	2.34	2.19	2.03	1.95	1.86	1.76	1.66	1.53	1.38
2.32	2.18	2.04	1.88	1.79	1.70	1.59	1.47	1.32	1.00

Source: *Biometrika Tables for Statisticians,* 3d. Ed., University College, London, 1966.

TABLE E

Median Rank Values

SAMPLE SIZE

RANK ORDER	1	2	3	4	5	6	7	8	9	10
1	50.0	29.3	20.6	15.9	12.9	10.9	9.4	8.3	7.4	6.7
2		70.7	50.0	38.6	31.4	26.4	22.8	20.1	18.0	16.2
3			79.4	61.4	50.0	42.1	36.4	32.1	28.6	25.9
4				84.1	68.6	57.9	50.0	44.0	39.3	35.5
5					87.1	73.6	63.6	56.0	50.0	45.2
6						89.1	77.2	67.9	60.7	54.8
7							90.6	79.9	71.4	64.5
8								91.7	82.0	74.1
9									92.6	83.8
10										93.3

SAMPLE SIZE

RANK ORDER	11	12	13	14	15	16	17	18	19	20
1	6.1	5.6	5.2	4.8	4.5	4.2	4.0	3.8	3.6	3.4
2	14.8	13.6	12.6	11.7	10.9	10.3	9.7	9.2	8.7	8.3
3	23.6	21.7	20.0	18.6	17.4	16.4	15.4	14.6	13.8	13.1
4	32.4	29.8	27.5	25.6	23.9	22.5	21.2	20.0	19.0	18.1
5	41.2	37.9	35.0	32.6	30.5	28.6	26.9	25.5	24.2	23.0
6	50.0	46.0	42.5	39.5	37.0	34.7	32.7	30.9	29.3	27.9
7	58.8	54.0	50.0	46.5	43.5	40.8	38.5	36.4	34.5	32.8
8	67.6	62.1	57.5	53.5	50.0	46.9	44.2	41.8	39.7	37.7
9	76.4	70.2	65.0	60.5	56.5	53.1	50.0	47.3	44.8	42.6
10	85.2	78.3	72.5	67.4	63.0	59.2	55.8	52.7	50.0	47.5
11	93.9	86.4	80.0	74.4	69.5	65.3	61.5	58.2	55.2	52.5
12		94.4	87.4	81.4	76.1	71.4	67.3	63.6	60.3	57.4
13			94.8	88.3	82.6	77.5	73.1	69.1	65.5	62.3
14				95.2	89.1	83.6	78.8	74.5	70.7	67.2
15					95.5	89.7	84.6	80.0	75.8	72.1
16						95.8	90.3	85.4	81.0	77.0
17							96.0	90.8	86.2	81.9
18								96.2	91.3	86.9
19									96.4	91.7
20										96.6

Reprinted with permission of ASQC Quality Press.

TABLE E (cont.)

SAMPLE SIZE

RANK ORDER	21	22	23	24	25	26	27	28	29	30
1	3.2	3.1	3.0	2.8	2.7	2.6	2.5	2.4	2.4	2.3
2	7.9	7.5	7.2	6.9	6.6	6.4	6.1	5.9	5.7	5.5
3	12.5	12.0	11.5	11.0	10.6	10.2	9.8	9.4	9.1	8.8
4	17.2	16.4	15.7	15.1	14.5	13.9	13.4	13.0	12.5	12.1
5	21.9	20.9	20.0	19.2	18.4	17.7	17.1	16.5	15.9	15.4
6	26.6	25.4	24.3	23.3	22.4	21.5	20.7	20.0	19.3	18.7
7	31.3	29.9	28.6	27.4	26.3	25.3	24.4	23.5	22.7	22.0
8	35.9	34.3	32.9	31.5	30.3	29.1	28.1	27.1	26.1	25.3
9	40.6	38.8	37.1	35.6	34.2	32.9	31.7	30.6	29.6	28.6
10	45.3	43.3	41.4	39.7	38.2	36.7	35.4	34.1	33.0	31.9
11	50.0	47.8	45.7	43.8	42.1	40.5	39.0	37.7	36.4	35.2
12	54.7	52.2	50.0	47.9	46.1	44.3	42.7	41.2	39.8	38.5
13	59.4	56.7	54.3	52.1	50.0	48.1	46.3	44.7	43.2	41.8
14	64.1	61.2	58.6	56.2	53.9	51.9	50.0	48.2	46.6	45.1
15	68.7	65.7	62.9	60.3	57.9	55.7	53.7	51.8	50.0	48.4
16	73.4	70.1	67.1	64.4	61.8	59.5	57.3	55.3	53.4	51.6
17	78.1	74.6	71.4	68.5	65.8	63.3	61.0	58.8	56.8	54.9
18	82.8	79.1	75.7	72.6	69.7	67.1	64.6	62.4	60.2	58.2
19	87.5	83.6	80.0	76.7	73.7	70.9	68.3	65.9	63.6	61.5
20	92.1	88.0	84.3	80.8	77.6	74.7	71.9	69.4	67.0	64.9
21	96.8	92.5	88.5	84.9	81.6	78.5	75.6	72.9	70.4	68.1
22		96.9	92.8	89.0	85.5	82.3	79.3	76.5	73.9	71.4
23			97.0	93.1	89.4	86.1	82.9	80.0	77.3	74.7
24				97.2	93.4	89.8	86.6	83.5	80.7	78.0
25					97.3	93.6	90.2	87.0	84.1	81.3
26						97.4	93.9	90.6	87.5	84.6
27							97.5	94.1	90.9	87.9
28								97.6	94.3	91.2
29									97.6	94.5
30										97.9

Reprinted with permission of ASQC Quality Press.

TABLE F

Factors for Control Charts for Variables $\overline{X}$, $\overline{Y}$, s, R: Normal Universe Factors for Computing Central Lines and 3-Sigma Control Limits

| | Chart for Averages | | | Chart for Standard Deviations | | | | | | Chart for Ranges | | | | | | |
| | Factors for Control Limits | | | Factors for Central Line | | Factors for Control Limits | | | | Factors for Central Line | | | Factors for Control Limits | | | |
Observations in Sample, n	A	A_2	A_3	c_4	$1/c_4$	B_3	B_4	B_5	B_6	d_2	$1/d_2$	d_3	D_1	D_2	D_3	D_4
2	2.121	1.880	2.659	0.7979	1.2533	0	3.267	0	2.606	1.128	0.8865	0.853	0	3.686	0	3.267
3	1.732	1.023	1.954	0.8862	1.1284	0	2.568	0	2.276	1.693	0.5907	0.888	0	4.358	0	2.574
4	1.500	0.729	1.628	0.9213	1.0854	0	2.266	0	2.088	2.059	0.4857	0.880	0	4.698	0	2.282
5	1.342	0.577	1.427	0.9400	1.0638	0	2.089	0	1.964	2.326	0.4299	0.864	0	4.918	0	2.114
6	1.225	0.483	1.287	0.9515	1.0510	0.030	1.970	0.029	1.874	2.534	0.3946	0.848	0	5.078	0	2.004
7	1.134	0.419	1.182	0.9594	1.0423	0.118	1.882	0.113	1.806	2.704	0.3698	0.833	0.204	5.204	0.076	1.924
8	1.061	0.373	1.099	0.9650	1.0363	0.185	1.815	0.179	1.751	2.847	0.3512	0.820	0.388	5.306	0.136	1.864
9	1.000	0.337	1.032	0.9693	1.0317	0.239	1.761	0.232	1.707	2.970	0.3367	0.808	0.547	5.393	0.184	1.816
10	0.949	0.308	0.975	0.9727	1.0281	0.284	1.716	0.276	1.669	3.078	0.3249	0.797	0.687	5.469	0.223	1.777
11	0.905	0.285	0.927	0.9754	1.0252	0.321	1.679	0.313	1.637	3.173	0.3152	0.787	0.811	5.535	0.256	1.744
12	0.866	0.266	0.886	0.9776	1.0229	0.354	1.646	0.346	1.610	3.258	0.3069	0.778	0.922	5.594	0.283	1.717
13	0.832	0.249	0.850	0.9794	1.0210	0.382	1.618	0.374	1.585	3.336	0.2998	0.770	1.025	5.647	0.307	1.693
14	0.802	0.235	0.817	0.9810	1.0194	0.406	1.594	0.399	1.563	3.407	0.2935	0.763	1.118	5.696	0.328	1.672
15	0.775	0.223	0.789	0.9823	1.0180	0.428	1.572	0.421	1.544	3.472	0.2880	0.756	1.203	5.741	0.347	1.653
16	0.750	0.212	0.763	0.9835	1.0168	0.448	1.552	0.440	1.526	3.532	0.2831	0.750	1.282	5.782	0.363	1.637
17	0.728	0.203	0.739	0.9845	1.0157	0.466	1.534	0.458	1.511	3.588	0.2787	0.744	1.356	5.820	0.378	1.622
18	0.707	0.194	0.718	0.9854	1.0148	0.482	1.518	0.475	1.496	3.640	0.2747	0.739	1.424	5.856	0.391	1.608
19	0.688	0.187	0.698	0.9862	1.0140	0.497	1.503	0.490	1.483	3.689	0.2711	0.734	1.487	5.891	0.403	1.597
20	0.671	0.180	0.680	0.9869	1.0133	0.510	1.490	0.504	1.470	3.735	0.2677	0.729	1.549	5.921	0.415	1.585
21	0.655	0.173	0.663	0.9876	1.0126	0.523	1.477	0.516	1.459	3.778	0.2647	0.724	1.605	5.951	0.425	1.575
22	0.640	0.167	0.647	0.9882	1.0119	0.534	1.446	0.528	1.448	3.819	0.2618	0.720	1.659	5.979	0.434	1.566
23	0.626	0.162	0.633	0.9887	1.0114	0.545	1.455	0.539	1.438	3.858	0.2592	0.716	1.710	6.006	0.443	1.557
24	0.612	0.157	0.619	0.9892	1.0109	0.555	1.445	0.549	1.429	3.895	0.2567	0.712	1.759	6.031	0.451	1.548
25	0.600	0.153	0.606	0.9896	1.0105	0.565	1.435	0.559	1.420	3.931	0.2544	0.708	1.8065	6.056	0.459	1.541

Reproduced from ASTM-STP 15D by permission of the American Society for Testing and Materials.

TABLE G

Gamma Function of Γ (x)

x	$\Gamma(x)$	x	$\Gamma(x)$
1.00	1.000000	1.26	0.904397
1.01	.994326	1.27	.902503
1.02	.988844	1.28	.900718
1.03	.983550	1.29	.899042
1.04	.978438	1.30	.897471
1.05	.973504	1.31	.896004
1.06	.968744	1.32	.894640
1.07	.964152	1.33	.893378
1.08	.959725	1.34	.892216
1.09	.955459	1.35	.891151
1.10	.951351	1.36	.890185
1.11	.947396	1.37	.889314
1.12	.943590	1.38	.888537
1.13	.939931	1.39	.887854
1.14	.936416	1.40	.887264
1.15	.933041	1.41	.886756
1.16	.929803	1.42	.886356
1.17	.926700	1.43	.886036
1.18	.923728	1.44	.885805
1.19	.920885	1.45	.885661
1.20	.918169	1.46	.885604
1.21	.915576	1.47	.885633
1.22	.913106	1.48	.885747
1.23	.910755	1.49	.885945
1.24	.908521	1.50	.886227
1.25	.906402	1.51	.886592

TABLE G (cont.)

x	$\Gamma(x)$	x	$\Gamma(x)$
1.52	.887037	1.78	.926227
1.53	.887568	1.79	.928767
1.54	.888178	1.80	.931384
1.55	.888868	1.81	.934076
1.56	.889639	1.82	.936845
1.57	.890490	1.83	.939690
1.58	.891420	1.84	.942612
1.59	.892428	1.85	.945611
1.60	.893515	1.86	.948687
1.61	.894681	1.87	.951840
1.62	.895924	1.88	.955071
1.63	.897244	1.89	.958379
1.64	.898642	1.90	.961766
1.65	.900117	1.91	.965231
1.66	.901668	1.92	.968774
1.67	.903296	1.93	.972397
1.68	.905001	1.94	.976099
1.69	.906782	1.95	.979881
1.70	.908639	1.96	.983743
1.71	.910572	1.97	.987685
1.72	.912581	1.98	.991708
1.73	.914665	1.99	.995813
1.74	.916826	2.00	1.000000
1.75	.919063		
1.76	.921375		
1.77	.923763		

For larger values of $\Gamma(x)$, $\Gamma(x+1) = x\Gamma(x)$.
EX: $\Gamma(2.3) = 1.3\ (.897471) = 1.166712$

Reprinted with permission of ASQC Quality Press.

BIBLIOGRAPHY

ASQC Statistics Division. *Glossary and Tables for Statistical Quality Control.* Milwaukee, WI: ASQC Quality Press, 1983.

Burr IW. *Applied Statistical Methods.* New York, NY: Academic Press, 1974.

Burr IW. *Statistical Quality Control Methods.* New York, NY: Marcel Dekker, Inc., 1976.

Dovich RA. *Reliability Statistics.* Milwaukee, WI: ASQC Quality Press, 1990.

Duncan AJ. *Quality Control and Industrial Statistics.* Homewood, IL: Irwin, 1986.

Grant EL, Leavenworth RS. *Statistical Quality Control.* New York, NY: McGraw-Hill Book Company, 1980.

Hansen BL. *Quality Control: Theory and Applications.* Englewood Cliffs, NJ: Prentice Hall, 1963.

Hicks CR. *Fundamental Concepts in the Design of Experiments.* New York, NY: Holt, Rinehart and Winston, 1982.

Juran JM, Gryna FM. *Juran's Quality Control Handbook.* New York, NY: McGraw-Hill, 1988.

Montgomery DC. *Design and Analysis of Experiments.* New York, NY: John Wiley and Sons, 1984.

Natrella MG. *Experimental Statistics.* Washington, DC: National Bureau of Standards Handbook 91, 1966.

Nelson LS. "Upper Confidence Limits on Average Number of Occurrences." *Journal of Quality Technology* 21, No. 1 (January 1989): 71-72.

Snedecor GW, Cochran WG. *Statistical Methods.* Ames, IA: Iowa State University Press, 1989.

Weingarten H. "Confidence Intervals for the Percent Nonconforming Based on Variables Data." *Journal of Quality Technology* 14, No. 4 (October 1982): 207-210.

INDEX